The History of

Church Street, before 1875;
Guildhall, Church and 'Eight Bells'

BENYON DE BEAUVOIR

1993

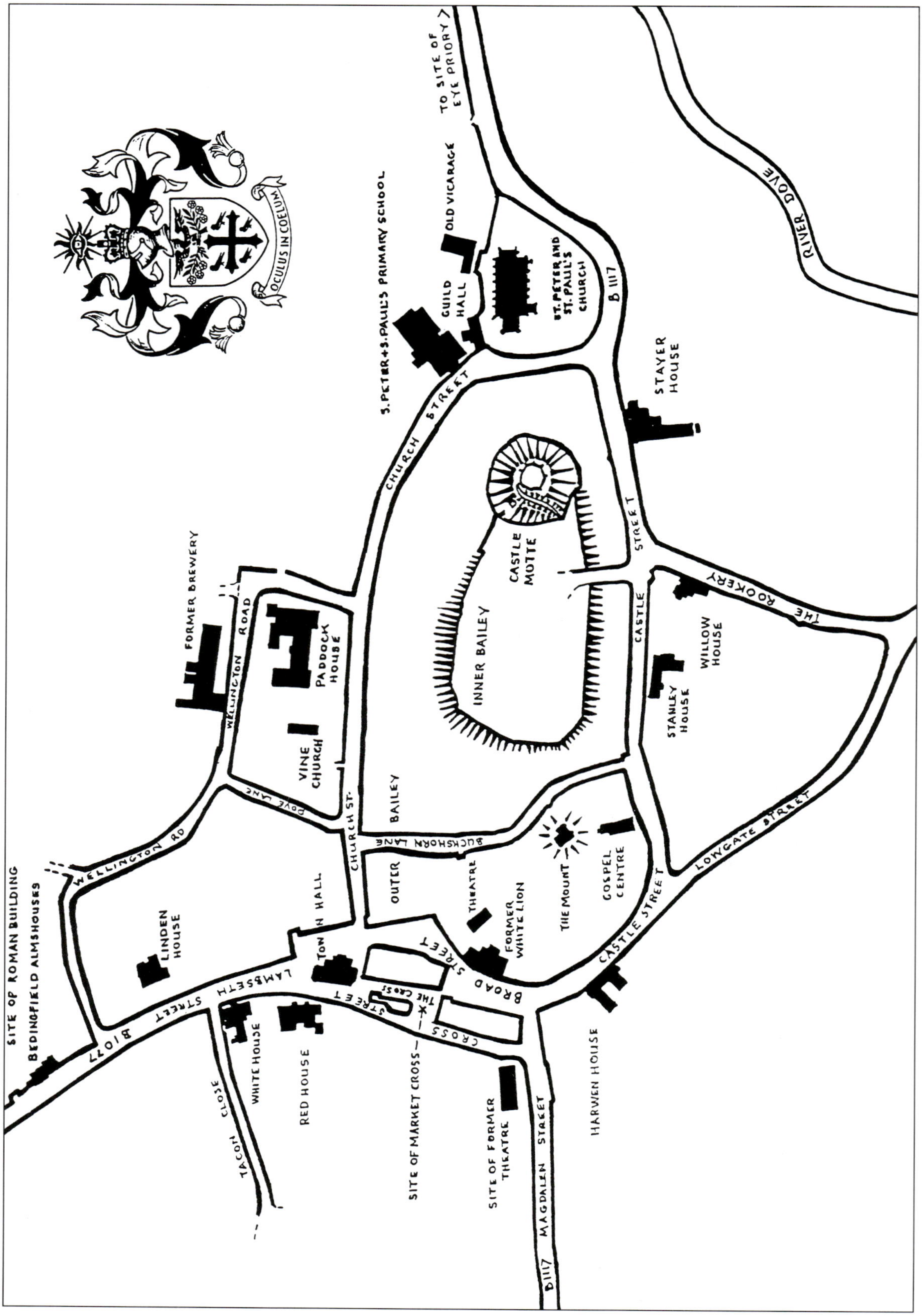
OCULUS IN COELUM
TO SITE OF EYE PRIORY
OLD VICARAGE
S. PETER + S. PAUL'S PRIMARY SCHOOL
GUILD HALL
ST. PETER AND ST. PAUL'S CHURCH
B 1117
RIVER DOVE
STAYER HOUSE
CHURCH STREET
CASTLE MOTTE
INNER BAILEY
CASTLE STREET
THE ROOKERY
WILLOW HOUSE
STANLEY HOUSE
FORMER BREWERY
WELLINGTON ROAD
PADDOCK HOUSE
VINE CHURCH
DOVE LANE
CHURCH ST.
OUTER BAILEY
BUCKSHORN LANE
THEATRE
FORMER WHITE LION
THE MOUNT
GOSPEL CENTRE
LOWGATE STREET
CASTLE STREET
SITE OF ROMAN BUILDING
BEDINGFIELD ALMSHOUSES
WELLINGTON RD
LINDEN HOUSE
TOWN HALL
LAMBSETH STREET
B1077
WHITE HOUSE
RED HOUSE
TACON CLOSE
THE CROSS
CROSS STREET
BROAD STREET
SITE OF MARKET CROSS
SITE OF FORMER THEATRE
MAGDALEN STREET
B1117
HARWEN HOUSE

Contents

Acknowledgements

My thanks have to go first and foremost to Jan and St. John Perry. To Jan for her enthusiasm and encouragement in the preparation of the text, for finding many of the illustrations from her friends in Eye, for co-ordinating the finance and seeing the book through to the press. To St. John for the mammoth task of typing the entire text whilst at Eye and Pouzauges, and for mastering my handwriting!

Tribute must also be paid to earlier researchers into the history of Eye. Elfrida Leaf broke much new ground in her thesis 'The History of Eye 1066–1603' (1935). The late Colonel John Busby collected a vast amount of historical material which now forms the core of the Local History Recorder's collection in the custody of Jan Perry. Much of the material was used in *A Guide to the History of Eye* (1981) by Dr. J. W. Arriens and Jan Perry. *The Borough of Eye Magazine* has proved a valuable source for tracing more recent events.

Thanks are also due to Dr. J. W. Arriens for the section on Notable Houses taken from *A Guide to the History of Eye;* to Moira Field of Wells-next-the-sea for help with the section on the Theatre; Dorothy Presswell of Exeter for help with the section on the Second World War; Ben Platts-Mills for information about the Town Moor and Peter Northeast of Rattlesden for advice on several sections, and for following up numerous obscure references at Cambridge University Library. Norman Sillman drew the Town Coat of Arms and one of the maps. The plan of the Priory was drawn by the late Peter Campbell.

Especial thanks must go to my wife Dorothy for her patience and encouragement during the researching and writing of this book.

Photographs and drawings have been reproduced with the kind permission of the Cleer Alger Trust for the photographs taken by Cleer S. Alger (1819-83) of Diss; Kate Campbell, Faith Legg, Joyce Muttock, Martin Crook of the Guildhall Book Room, Aerofilms, Eye Primary School, Hartismere Hospital, the Suffolk Record Office, the Trustees of the British Museum and Norfolk Museums Service (Norwich Castle Museum). Eye Town Council kindly gave permission to reproduce the Town Coat of Arms.

The following organisations and people have generously made gifts or loans towards the cost of publication: Eye Show Ltd., Eye Town Council, Fibropower, Pharmaco-L.S.R., Sovereign Chicken, Mr. & Mrs. M. Channon, Dr. & Mrs. J. Dixon, Mr. & Mrs. A. Evitt, Mr. & Mrs.D. Fisher, Mr. H. Grisewood, Mr. & Mrs. D. Jukes, Mr. & Mrs. R. Krawiec, Mr. & Mrs. G. Maynard, Mr. & Mrs. C. Michell, Mrs. A. Renshaw, Mr. & Mrs. N. Sillman, Dr. & Mrs. Vicary.

Introduction

From my earliest years I can remember my maternal Grandmother Ada Paine (née Green) talking about her childhood in Eye before the First World War. Lady Bateman of Brome Hall; Sir Thomas Tacon, Brewer, Mayor and County Councillor; Harold Warnes, Secretary of the Eye Gas Company; Arthur Till the Postmaster for whom she worked as a maid; Dr.Edgar Barnes, for whom her brother Walter worked as a chauffeur, and Frederick Bray, the headmaster of the National School where she received a silver and five bronze attendance medals, were as familiar to me as the members of my own family

Ada was one of seven children of Jane (née Leeder, 1857-1929) and Robert Green (1862-1910), and was born in the Gas House in Magdalen Street, where Robert worked for the Eye Gas Company. His job was to tend the retorts in the adjacent red brick 'Retort House', and to light and extinguish all the street lights in Eye. At the time of his death he had been employed at the Gas Works for 30 years; been a member of the Odd Fellows Lodge for 30 years; a member of the Eye Volunteers for 25 years; and a member of the Fire Brigade for 8 years.

My real link with Eye began in 1986 when I was invited by the University of Cambridge Board of Extra Mural Studies, at the instigation of Miss Joan Thompson, to run a 20 week course on the History of Eye, at Hartismere High School. The 20 weeks turned into 40 during the winters of 1986-7 and 1987-8, as together we explored many aspects of the locality.

I was delighted when Jan Perry, your enthusiastic Local History Recorder, invited me to write this History of Eye, much of which is based on the research and discoveries of those two years. In attempting to cover a period from the Romans to the present day, many things have had to be touched on lightly. Where more detailed research has been published, references are given in the footnotes which will also give access to all the manuscript and printed sources used in compiling this book.

Eye like every other community has its own distinct history and myths. I have tried to trace and interpret the events of the past, omit the myths, and hopefully not create any new ones of my own!

October 1993

Clive Paine
12, Hardwick Lane
Bury St Edmunds

Thatched cottage in Church Street, and the keep erected by Sir Edward Kerrison in 1844, including the tower built as a residence for his batman.

The Name and Site of Eye

The name Eye derives from the Old English word for an island, which can also be found in other local place names such as Kersey, Lindsey and Bawdsey.[1]

The earliest description of the site of Eye was recorded by John Leyland in the 1530s. 'Eye in Saxon signifies an island, whence also the town derives its name, because it was, as it were, entirely surrounded by water. And though it is not the case at the present day to the same extent, yet the surrounding neighbourhood is so marshy, and in winter so covered with water, that it is a clear proof that once it was a stagnant marsh'.[2]

The settlement at Eye was situated on the island of higher ground surrounded by marshland, part of which became the Town Moor. The island is formed by the low lying water meadows of the River Dove on the east and south-east, the stream flowing from Yaxley into the Dove on the north, and the Town Moor on the south and west. Norman Scarfe has suggested that the Moor may be partly artificial, like the mere at Framlingham, and created as the result of quarrying the earth needed to heighten the centre of the island as the castle.[3]

The low lying land was crossed by causeways to Moor Hall, Park Farm and Ludgate hamlet; the River Dove by Bolser, Abbey and Kings Bridges; the river from Yaxley by Lambseth Bridge; and the watercourse through the Moor by Magdalen or Spittal Bridge. The tenant of Eye Priory in 1598 had to maintain '. . . the causeway leading towards the church, and five timber bridges namely the three Abbey Bridges, Largate Bridge and Botsford Bridge'.[4]

Leyland also recorded that 'anciently laden boats used to come to the town from Chromatico (Cromer) or from a bay in the vicinity. This is evident from the fact that when the monks of Eye were cleaning ditches they found ships' rudders, cables smeared with pitch and other items of boating equipment. Now (1530s) boats cannot come beyond Burston, which is 12 miles from Eye'.[5]

Neither the statement about Cromer nor Burston makes any sense, as there is no direct river route from Cromer to Burston or Eye. Cromer is not the place to start from in order to reach Eye! However, the River Waveney from Lowestoft or Great Yarmouth would give access to Eye via the River Dove. An alternative route would have been from the Wash via the Rivers Little Ouse, Waveney and Dove.

Perhaps Leyland having heard of the discovery of 'boating equipment' sought an explanation, which he thought, or was told, was the link with Cromer. But finding such remains should not be unexpected in a place like Eye surrounded by marshland, whose inhabitants would have used boats for transport and fishing, and who would have built landing stages at the edge of the marsh.

The centre of the island site formed the base of the castle built by William Malet 1066–71.[6] The castle motte occupied the east end, with an inner and outer bailey stretching to the west. The elliptical plan of the castle site determined the future shape of the town of Eye. Church Street follows the curve of the northern ditch, Castle Street the southern, with the market place, established by William Malet 1066–71, situated on the west, at the entrance to the outer bailey. The site of the church which pre-dated the castle, is to the east of the castle ditch. A roughly circular-shaped churchyard usually indicates an early Christian site, and there was certainly a church at Eye in 1066.

The Priory, founded by Robert Malet 1086–7,[7] stands a quarter of a mile further east beyond the River Dove.

Eye Park, which lay to the south of the castle, was probably laid out by Robert Malet 1071–86, and later enclosed c.1200 by Henry, Duke of Brabant and Louvaine, and Lord of the Honour of Eye.[8] The present Eye Park House stands on the probable site of the former lodge in the centre of the Park.

Archaeological Finds

There have been a few paleolithic, mesolithic and neolithic finds in the parish of Eye, although nothing significant enough to indicate a settlement.

A Late Bronze Age 'founders hoard' dating from c.1100–700 B.C., was discovered near the River Dove, to the south-west of Eye Park House, in 1979. The hoard consisted of a complete axe and three fragments of socketed axes, and a broken chisel.[1] This is one of five such hoards to come from the parishes around Eye near the River Dove, and may indicate that the bronze smiths were using the ready supply of timber on the heavy clay land of High Suffolk.

The earliest evidence of an actual settlement at Eye comes from the Roman period. The present A140 was laid out as a Roman road from Colchester to Caister-by-Norwich, via the small town settlement of Scole, which was then called Villa Faustini. In 1857, the remains of what is now thought to be a third or fourth century corn drying kiln, used in the malting process, was discovered, indicating the presence of a farmstead settlement.[2] Because the structure of this type of kiln is similar to that of a hypocaust, the site was originally interpreted as being a Roman Villa.[3] The field in which this find was made was called Camping Close, and lies between Wellington Road and the stream, behind the Bedingfield Almshouses.

A hoard of over 600 Roman gold coins dating from c.364–410 was found in a lead box at Clint Farm in 1781.[4] Until the 'Hoxne Treasure' was discovered in 1992, this hoard was the most valuable ever found in Suffolk. The coins were probably buried for safety at the end of the Roman occupation of Britain by a person who lived locally, knew the area well and hoped to relocate the coins at a later date. Another group of six Roman coins dating from c.365 was found on the west side of Lowgate Street in 1965.[5]

An early Anglo-Saxon pagan burial ground was discovered in 1818, on the west side of the River Dove at Waterloo Plantation.[6] Within three or four days two labourers uncovered 150 burial urns, containing calcined bones, in an area of 120 square yards. Some of the urns also contained items of brass, iron and bone, including a triangular comb, carved knife, small shears, two pairs of tweezers, a set of toilet implements and two bone buttons. The large number of urns used indicates the presence of a nearby Anglo-Saxon settlement. Both Bronze Age Beaker pottery, and Romano-British pottery have been found near the cemetery to the west of Waterloo Plantation.

The Eye cemetery is one of three discovered adjacent to the River Dove and would suggest that the river valley had been colonised, probably via the river Waveney, during the mid-5th to 7th centuries.

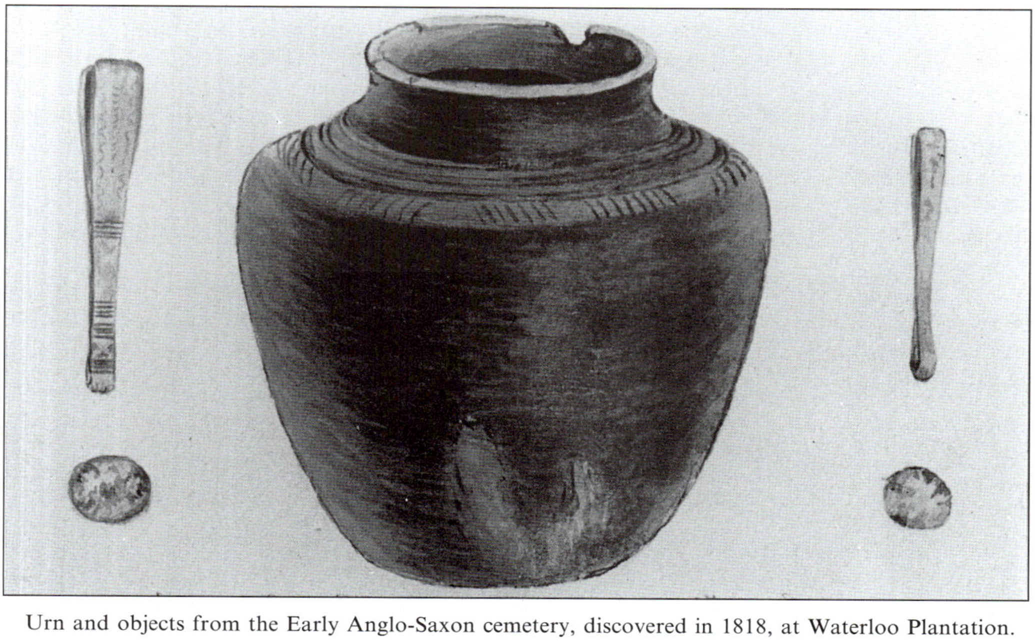

Urn and objects from the Early Anglo-Saxon cemetery, discovered in 1818, at Waterloo Plantation.

Norman Eye

Before the Norman Conquest, Eye was one of the numerous holdings of Edric of Laxfield, the third largest landholder in Suffolk after King Edward the Confessor and the Abbot of Bury St. Edmunds. It is quite possible that Laxfield rather than Eye was the headquarters of Edric's territories. There certainly seems to be no clear evidence that there was a fortified mound in Eye before 1066. At the Conquest Edric was displaced, and all his lands distributed amongst the Norman Lords. William Malet had the largest share in Suffolk and Norfolk, and was also granted land in six other counties.

William Malet came from Graville Sainte Honorine between Le Havre and Harfleur in Normandy. He fought with distinction at Hastings, and was entrusted with the burial of King Harold Godwinson at Battle.

At Eye, William was responsible for heightening the island site, constructing the castle, and establishing the market between 1066 and 1071. William is believed to have died fighting against Hereward the Wake in the Fens in 1071. Domesday Book records that '. . . he went into the marsh' and that '. . . he went on the King's service, where he died'. For some reason William's son Robert did not inherit all his father's lands, many of which were given to other Norman landholders. In 1086 Robert's estate comprised land in 208 parishes of which 137 were in Suffolk.

Robert was Sheriff of Suffolk 1071–c.1080 and in 1075–6 was responsible for suppressing the rebellion of Ralph, Earl of Norfolk. He seems to have been deprived of the Honour by William Rufus, in favour of Roger the Poitevin, after 1087. Robert returned to his Normandy estates, possibly because he felt more loyalty to William's brother, Robert Duke of Normandy. With the accession of Henry I in 1100 he returned to England, was restored to the Lordship of Eye, and became one of the King's inner circle of advisers. At the time of his death, at the battle of Tinchebrai in Normandy in 1106, he held the office of High Chamberlain to the King.[2] At Eye, Robert was responsible for founding the Benedictine Priory of St. Peter 1086–7, and probably for creating the park as a hunting preserve in 1086.

The Domesday details for Eye reveal a large agricultural settlement, with a population of c.700, in which there had been considerable changes between 1066 and 1086.[3] The number of plough teams had fallen from 36½ to 24½ in 1086, and the 12 slaves of 1066, probably used to work the manorial ploughs, had gone by 1086. The area of woodland, measured by the number of pigs the woodland could support, had declined from 136 pigs, or about 400 acres, to 69 pigs or about 250 acres.[4]

The building of the castle and the creation of the park may have accounted for some of these changes. A highly successful market had been established in 1066–71, with 25 trading burgesses living around the market place. All this evidence points to the growing urbanisation of Eye, as the military and administrative headquarters of the Honour of Eye.

Eye Castle

There is no archaeological or documentary evidence that there was a castle, or a raised mound, at Eye before the Conquest. The townsmen of Eye told John Leyland that the '. . . castle was destroyed by the command of William the Norman'.[1] No doubt they were trying to explain why there was so little of the structure left in the 1530s. Perhaps the folk lore remembered the confiscation of Malet land after 1087 by William Rufus, and assumed that the castle had been demolished.

However, evidence from the Domesday entry for Hoxne records that '. . . William Malet made his castle at Eye'.[2] As William died in 1071, the typical Norman castle with motte, inner and outer baileys must have been constructed during the five years following the Norman conquest. Unusually there was a second smaller motte, which may have been constructed as a watchtower, roughly in the centre of the outer bailey, which survives in Buckshorn Lane behind the Gospel Centre.

Excavation in 1978 showed that '. . . the natural hill had been first surrounded with a bank, presumably upcast from the bailey ditch, and the whole interior had been raised with layers of imported soil 6–9 feet thick'.[3] The motte is 160 feet wide at the base, and stands 50 feet above the bailey on the east, and 40 feet on the west side. The inner bailey is 420 feet long, east to west, and 250 feet wide. The curving western end is marked by the building line of the present houses, which were designed with buttresses to imitate the castle walls, even though there is no evidence of a castle wall at this point! The motte and inner bailey are encompassed by the outer bailey, measuring 1,070 feet long and 420 feet wide.

The only stonework parts of the castle to survive are the foundations of a tower on the north-west side of the motte and about 85 feet of the northern curtain wall of the inner bailey, ranging from 7–18 feet in height. The 'castle keep' is a Victorian folly erected in 1844, which '. . . may at least in part be founded on the original walls of the keep'.[4]

The main event in the history of Eye came in 1173, during the rebellion against Henry II by Prince Henry, Hugh Bigod Earl of Norfolk, and the Earl of Leicester. There had been a power struggle in Norfolk and Suffolk between the King and Hugh Bigod since the 1150s. The King held castles at Eye, Haughley, Walton and Orford, spending £1,400 on building the latter in 1165–73. Bigod had castles at Framlingham and Bungay, where a new keep was begun in 1165. Prince Henry promised Bigod the Castle and Honour of Eye as a reward for his support in the rebellion.

At Eye various repairs were made to the castle 1164–9. In 1173 nearly £21 was spent '. . . in building work of the castle of Eye and repairing the old palisades and two new palisades and ditches and for carriage and stone . . .'.[5] This may have included the two towers, with two narrow chambers in between, on the inside of the northern curtain wall of the inner bailey. It is possible that the chambers were used as 'the prison within the castle' so often referred to in contemporary documents. This complex was excavated in 1987–8 and dated to the late 12th century.[6] It may of course date from 1175 and form part of the repair work following the rebellion. The 1173 accounts also show that £30 was spent in garrisoning, and nearly £37 in provisioning the castle.[7]

The rebellion started with an attack on Walton castle on the 23 September 1173 and ended when Bigod asked for a truce in late October. During the month-long rebellion, Haughley castle had been destroyed, Eye attacked and damaged, and the Earl of Leicester's army of Flemings defeated at Fornham St Genevieve.

As a result of the attack on Eye much repair work was required. The 1174–5 accounts show expenditure on three new palisades, raising walls, rebuilding three burnt barns and two cattle sheds, repairing two bridges, remaking the divisions in the fishpond, and the purchase of 60 lances. Apart from the stockade and walls, the other damaged buildings may have been in the town rather that the castle.

The account also records over £6 spent on replacing the stock of the manor of Eye 'which was lost through war', and £94 of income lost '. . . for waste by war, of corn in the demesnes burnt and carried off by Earl Hugh this year and last year'.[8] Further repairs were made 1178–82 to the palisades and to the buildings in the castle '. . . destroyed in time of war'.[9] By the end of this phase of repair and rebuilding Eye castle was probably at the peak of its development.

In 1192 King Richard I feared that a rebellion would be led by his brother John. Amongst the defensive measures taken throughout the country, a garrison of 6 knights, 12 foot sergeants and 7 horses were to be maintained at Eye.

During the Barons war of 1265 the castle was sacked, and probably never regained its former security and status after this event.

As early as 1215 there is mention of the 'King's Prison at Eye'.[10] In 1315–16 repairs were carried out to a room in the goal which had been damaged in a gale, which also damaged the gate and walls of the castle and buildings in the bailey. From the early 14th century the 'custody of the castle and the prison within the castle' went together.[11]

In 1556 the 'Aye Dongeon' held the Protestant martyrs, Adam Foster, John Denny and Edmund Pole of Mendlesham, Thomas Spicer of Winston and Robert Lawson, while they awaited trial. Foster and Lawson were burnt at Bury; Spicer, Denny and Pole at Beccles in May and June 1556.[12]

Although the prison continued to be used until the early 17th century, evidence from the 1987–8 excavation suggested a period of demolition or destruction of most of the castle buildings in the 14th century. When John Leyland visited Eye in the 1530s he noted 'Eye once had a noble castle next to the marshes, but now there is only a watchtower, and ruins of walls in some places'.[13] Some of these remains must have been gradually demolished as the castle would have made a good quarry for stone. Tom Martin recorded that 'Nicholas alias Trooper Todd was killed in pulling down some of the walls in 1706'.[14]

A deed of 1591 records that a windmill had been built on the 'castle hill' in 1561–2 by Nicholas Cutler, on the orders of Lord Cornwallis.[15] A windmill remained on the mound until 1844, when Sir Edward Kerrison had it demolished and built a crenellated imitation of a castle keep. David Davy, the Suffolk antiquarian visited Eye in June 1844, and recorded in his Journal. 'Passing the Castle Hill I found a lofty scaffold erected and operations going on, which upon enquiry, I heard were the building of a castle on the top by Sir Edward Kerrison. The structure was to be of white brick formed in moulds for the purpose, and to cover the whole top of the hill, about 12 or 14 feet seemed to be all then finished.'[16]

A house was built within the castle shell for Sir Edward's batman, who had saved his life at Waterloo. Sometime before 1907 a museum of bygones and natural history was established in the house until c.1917. Sir Edward's castle wall was severely damaged in a storm in early 1965.

The western half of the inner bailey contained the parish workhouse from the 18th century until 1916, part of which was the Borough Gaol from 1817–37. The buildings were partly demolished in the 1920s, and the remainder converted into council houses. The entire site was cleared in 1979 and the award winning council houses built along the western end. Eye National School occupied the eastern end of the inner bailey from 1839–1987, although the buildings ceased to be part of the Church Aided Primary School in 1979.

The castle remained in private hands until 1923 when it was given to the Borough, and became an Ancient Monument in 1932. It is now the property of Mid-Suffolk District Council, who are preparing the site as part of a projected Heritage Centre.

The Mill, Eye, Suffolk, watercolour painting by John Sell Cotman (1782–1842). (Original at Castle Museum, Norwich.)

The Honour of Eye

An Honour consisted of holdings of manors and land, granted by the King to one of his chief barons, in return for the provision of a certain number of knights whenever the King needed them for military service. The Lord of the Honour would, in his turn, grant many of the manors and lands to under-tenants, some of whom would be knights. The Honour of Eye was originally assessed at 90½ Knights' Fees, and increased to 104¾ in the early 12th century.[1] This meant that the Lord could be called upon to provide that number of knights for the King's military service.

As time went by, the provision of this military service was commuted to money rents called scutage (shield service) but the holdings were still reckoned as numbers, or fractions of Knights' Fees. For example in 1300, Edwardstone was held by 12 Knights' Fees, whereas Huntingfield and Westleton were held by 1¼ and ¼ Knights' Fees respectively.[2]

Because the chief place or 'caput', of the Honour was a castle, the Lord's under-tenants also had to provide 'castle-guard' for the protection of the castle for 40 days each year. By the 13th century this duty had also generally been commuted to a money payment, called castleguard or castleward.

The under-tenants and peasants owed feudal service to their Lords, and also to the Lord of the Honour. For example the tenants at Brundish, Tannington, Badingham, Dennington, Laxfield and Stradbroke, had to repair part of the palisade around Eye Park, and part of the causeways leading to the castle.[3] Free tenants also owed service by 'socage and suite of court' for their holdings within the Honour. This required money payments and attendance at the annual 'suit roll' at the Tourn.

The Honour of Eye was a widely scattered grouping of manors and land holdings spread over eight counties, and was one of the largest estates in England after 1066. The bulk of the land was in Suffolk and Norfolk and before 1066 had been the estate of Edric of Laxfield. At the time of Domesday Book in 1086 some of the land had been granted to other magnates, following the death of William Malet in 1071. The Honour, now held by Robert Malet, comprised land in 137 parishes in Suffolk, 35 in Yorkshire, 22 in Norfolk, 6 in Lincolnshire, 4 in Essex, 2 in Nottinghamshire, 1 in Rutland and 1 in Surrey, although the size of the individual holdings ranged from a few acres to entire parishes.

By the Domesday assessment of caracates, borates, woodland and acres the total area must have been at least 75,000 acres, of which 47,000 were in Suffolk. Robert Malet was the second largest landowner in Suffolk, after the Abbot of St Edmundsbury. The Suffolk holdings lay in 27% of the total number of parishes, mainly in High Suffolk and the coastal Sandlings. It has been suggested that the term "High Suffolk' may have derived from 'Eye Suffolk', the area of the Honour.[4] Eye with its castle, church, priory and market was the administrative centre of the Honour.

Because of its vast extent, the territory of the Honour was divided, from an early date, into two administrative units called Bailiwicks and Tourns. The surviving evidence comes mainly from the period 1594–1787, and relates to 74 parishes with freehold tenants, which represents 54% of 137 Domesday parishes. The detailed records of the manorial Castle Guard payments have not survived. However in 1787 when the surviving series of records cease, both Castle Guard rents and fees from freeholders were still being collected.

Each of the 8 Bailiwicks was administrated by its own Bailiff. The Bailiwicks ranged in size from 4 to 16 parishes, some of which were tightly grouped, while others were scattered over a wide area. For example the Bailiwick of Strange comprised 14 parishes in Blything Hundred, while the Bailiwick of Chamberlain comprised 8 parishes in Hoxne Hundred, 6 in Wilford, 1 in Bosmere and 1 in Stow.[5]

The Bailiffs, who had heraldic sounding names, had to collect the Castle Guard rents on behalf of the Lord, and to attend the Court Baron of the Honour, '. . . with a white rod as a sign of their office'.[6] Bailiff Chamberlain, possibly named after the office, was responsible for manorial holdings in 16 parishes; Bailiff Strange in 14 parishes; Vaux in 13; Turge, possibly named after a landholding in Rishangles, in 8; Eyre in 8; Parker, possibly originally the Park Keeper, in 6; Sudden, a hamlet of Eye, in 5; Berne in 4, and Burgh was the junior Bailiff for Eye.

By the 18th century, the office of Bailiff had become a sinecure held by nobles and gentry who acted through paid deputies. For example in 1743 the Earl of Leicester was Bailiff Strange;

Aerial view of Eye c.1975. Shows the outline of castle baileys, now marked by Church, Broad and Castle Streets. The former workhouse in the inner bailey was demolished in 1979. Abbey Farm is in the distance.

Admiral Vernon of Nacton was Bailiff Parker, and Lord Cornwallis, Lord of the Honour of Eye, was also Bailiff Berne.[7]

A parallel administrative unit to the Bailiwick was the Tourn, or circuit, during which the Court Leet and View of Frankpledge were held. Adjacent parishes within the Honour were grouped into 6 Tourns of between 7 and 18 parishes each, and called after the meeting place. The Honorial Tourns may be of a later date than the Bailiwicks, or perhaps superseded the Tourns of the Sheriff of Suffolk. In the Hundred Rolls of 1275, there are references to the Bailiffs of the Honour holding '. . . a new tourn at Boxlowe, in Blything Hundred, and elsewhere at their will, which should have been held by the Sheriff', and that in Hartismere Hundred the Steward of Eye had '. . . held a tourn by year in the bailiwick'.[8]

The bulk of parishes of a particular Tourn usually lay in the same Hundred. Deering (in Dunwich) Tourn comprised 11 parishes in Blything Hundred; Brundish, 12 parishes in Hoxne; Buxlow (in Knodishall), 13 in Plomsgate and 1 in Blything; Finningham, 16 in Hartismere, 1 in Bosmere and 1 in Stow; Debenham, 4 in Hartismere, 2 in Hoxne and 1 in Bosmere and 1 in Thredling, all of which were adjacent; and the more scattered Alderton in south-east Suffolk had 9 parishes in Wilford, 2 in Carlford and 1 in Loes Hundreds. At the Tourn the free tenants appeared to acknowledge they held land or tenements '. . . of the Turne in free and common soccage, by fealtie, sute of Court, and the service of one knight of the Turne'; paid their customary dues; and heard causes within the jurisdiction of the Court Leet, such as obstructing the highway, allowing ditches to overflow, and illegally grazing cattle on road verges.

The tenants of the Honour were granted privileges of exemption from various tolls and payments, relating to travel and trading throughout the whole kingdom. These were stallage, a payment for erecting stalls at markets and fairs; chiminage, a toll to pass through a forest; pontage, a toll for crossing a bridge; pavage levied for paving highways and streets; picage, a payment for breaking the ground in setting up booths and stalls at a fair; murage, levied for building or repairing town walls; and passage, a charge levied on travellers.

The earliest surviving grant of these privileges was made in 1381, by William de Ufford, Duke of Suffolk and Lord of the Honour. This, however, renewed earlier grants made by Ufford's ancestors, and other lords of the Honour, to their tenants '. . . as they used to be time out of mind'. There is evidence to show that the privileges were confirmed in 1384, 1385, 1401 and 1439.[9] Certificates were issued to tenants wishing to claim the privileges, by the Steward and Keeper of the Seal of the Honour of Eye. For example a certificate was given to William Meys of Stowmarket in 1445, who was a tenant at Thornham Magna and sometimes lived there, and '. . . is therefore to be held quit of the said dues and burdens'.[10]

From the death of Robert Malet in 1106 until 1697 the Honour, and the title Lord of the Honour of Eye, was held by Kings, Queens, Princes, various noble families including the Earls and Dukes of Suffolk, and Archbishop Thomas à Becket. The Dukes of Brabant and Louvaine were Lords 1198–1230; the de Ufford family of Parham, Earls of Suffolk 1344-82; the de la Poles of Wingfield, Earls and Dukes of Suffolk 1398–1450 and 1463–1513; Charles Brandon, Duke of Suffolk, husband of Mary Tudor, was Lord of the Honour of Eye 1514-38.[11]

From 1538 until 1697, with the exception of the Commonwealth, the Honour was held by members of the Royal Family. King William III, the last Royal Lord of the Honour, granted it in 1697 to Charles 3rd Lord Cornwallis of Brome,[12] whose family had been Stewards since at least 1632.[13] The Cornwallis family, who had been granted the title of Lord Cornwallis of Eye in 1661, continued to be Lords of the Honour until the death of the last Marquis in 1823. The title then passed to the Kerrisons (1823–86) the Bateman-Hanbury family and their Trustees (1886–1923). The Lordship was purchased by Adolphus Maskell of Chelmsford (1924–37) and on his death was held by Trustees, who sold it in 1984 to Donald Wilson of Cheltenham. The present Baroness, or Lady of the Honour, is Lady Urquhart, Baroness of Eye, who lives at Topcroft in Norfolk, and in 1993 purchased the Lordship of the Honour, and the Lordships of the Manors of Eye Hall otherwise Eye Priory, Eye Sokemere, Cranley Hall in Eye, Hoxne Hall with the Priory and Eye Thelnetham.

There is no evidence to show that any of the Lords of the Honour lived in Eye or at the Castle. All the medieval Lords were Royalty or nobles with grander castles and houses elsewhere. The Earls and Dukes of Suffolk lived at Parham, Wingfield and Westhorp, although there is circumstantial evidence to show that Charles Brandon stayed either at the Priory, or at the grand brick building to the west of the Priory. The important factors for the Lords were the status, the income and the local power base that the Honour conferred.

The Honour was administered on behalf of the absent Lord by the Steward or Bailiff of Eye. He was assisted by two paid officials, the under-steward, or junior bailiff, and the Chamberlain who probably did most of the routine day to day work.[14] The Steward, or his deputies, were responsible for holding the Court Baron to enforce the manorial bye laws, and to hear disputes between the tenants.

The Stewardship was often held by men who, like the Lord, also did not live in Eye. For example Sir Henry Heydon who was Steward in 1500 lived at Franconsthorp near Holt in Norfolk.[15] The castle was supervised by a Constable, Bailiff or Custodian, whose office was sometimes also taken by the Steward. The Lords often granted a lease of the Honour to the Steward, in exchange for a portion of the income. Two of the Tudor Stewards were local men; Sir Nicholas Bacon of Redgrave, and Charles Cutler, one of the first M.P.s for Eye in 1571.

The castle was the administrative headquarters of the Honour in the early days, and as it fell into disuse, and was reduced to a prison in the 14th century, other accommodation may have been sought. It was most probable that by c.1500 the administrative centre had moved to the splendid brick building at the Priory.

View from the Castle motte, showing the Church, Guildhall, Old Vicarage, and The Abbey on the site of the Priory in the distance.

The Church of St Peter and St Paul

An excellent guide is available from the church, and the following paragraphs are by way of a supplement to its contents.

There has been a church in Eye at least since 1066, which later became part of Robert Malet's endowment of the Priory. The semi-circular churchyard is indicative of an early Christian site.

The present building dates from the 14th century Decorated period of architecture, which survives in the chancel arch, the arches into the chancel chapels and the tomb recess in the north aisle. A 13th-century Early English doorway was re-used from the earlier building as the south door of the aisle.

In the 15th century there was a period of both rebuilding and new building. The nave arcades were renewed and the clerestory in the nave and chancel constructed in the Perpendicular style. The aisles had Perpendicular windows inserted, and may even have been rebuilt. Surviving wills show that between 1470 and 1484, at least £13 1s 8d was bequeathed to the 'reparacion' and 'emendation' of the church;[1] in 1477, £3 6s 8d for leading the roof of the north aisle;[2] and in 1487 a massive bequest of £13 6s 8d was given to pave the church with marble.[3]

There is no evidence of an earlier tower, and bequests were made to the 'new tower' 1453–79. Impetus was given to the building work and fund raising in 1454 by Alice, widow of William de la Pole (d.1450), Duke of Suffolk and Lord of the Honour of Eye. Alice granted £13 6s 8d '. . . to the new work of the tower there (Eye), to have a perpetual memorial among the tenants of the Lord there, for the soul of her Lord William late Duke of Suffolk, late her husband, and for the good estate of the said Duchess and John their son.'[4]

Between 1453 and 1469 at least £18 had been bequeathed specifically for the new tower by the Duchess of Suffolk and the townspeople of Eye, plus 12 cartloads of flints, and malt and wheat for a church ale.

A mid-16th century note in Eye Town Book 'Z', records details from a now lost churchwarden's account, made in 1470 during the final phase of fund raising and construction.[5] In 1470, the churchwardens having only £1 6s 2d in hand, raised over £40 '. . . partly with the plowgh (collections made on Plough Monday in January), partly in church ales (similar to church fetes), partly in legacies given that way (amounting to at least £5 10s in the period 1470–79), but chiefly of the frank and devoute hartes of the people.' With this income the churchwardens '. . . dyd byld up the steple and wer at charges with the bells ther . . .' Mr Hynnyngham had provided most of the flints, and the Prior had lent the churchwardens 25$^1/_2$ hundredweight of lead.

All the evidence points to a period of 20–25 years of building work, which would have been quite usual for a church tower. The work probably started in 1454 with the grant of the Dowager Duchess, and the belfry stage with flushwork decoration, bells and roof was started in 1470. The work seems to have been completed by 1479 when Robert Anyell, a benefactor of Eye and a churchwarden in 1470, requested to be buried in the tower.[6] The result of the fund raising and bequests was '. . . one of the wonders of Suffolk, 101 feet tall and panelled in flushwork from foot to parapet.'[7]

On the south side of the parapet an angel holds a coat of arms, which has usually been attributed to John de la Pole, second Duke of Suffolk and Lord of Eye who died in 1491. However, the intention of the 1454 grant was that the tower should commemorate William, the first Duke of Suffolk who died in 1450. Indeed the arms are those of de la Pole (3 leopards' faces) and Burghersh (a lion rampant, with a double tail), for William de la Pole and Alice née Chaucer whose mother was Maud Burghersh of Witnesham. Their son John married Elizabeth Plantaganet, sister of Edward IV and Richard III in 1460. If the arms were John's, then surely de la Pole would have been quartered with the arms of England, as on the font at nearby Hoxne, and not with those of his grandmother.

There is no documentary evidence for the building of the south porch. However, the base has a series of flushwork panels including IHS for Jesus, a pot of lilies for the Virgin Mary, and a series of initials. It is probable that these initials, as at Blythburgh, are from the townspeople who gave money in their lifetime, to start the construction of the porch. The spandrils of the west window each have the de la Pole leopard face, and on the south-west buttress there are five heraldic devices, which provide further clues to the building of the porch above the base level.

On the central facet of the buttress are the arms of de la Pole quartered with Burghersh; either side is a chained stag, as a supporter to the arms; further left is de la Pole; and to the right is Burghersh. The chained stag was one of the supporters of the Royal Arms of Edward IV (1461–83), and its use on the porch may indicate that it was built during his reign. Because the de la Pole arms are not quartered with Plantaganet, but supported by the Plantaganet stag, it is possible that Dame Alice, rather than her son John, was responsible for building the porch. Perhaps Dame Alice gave money specifically for the porch as a further memorial of her husband, herself and their son John, now married to Elizabeth Plantaganet. If the porch was built in Dame Alice's lifetime then the construction period would be narrowed to 1460–75. Whatever the actual explanation is, all the evidence points to the period of major reconstruction throughout the church in the 1470s.

Between the south clerestory windows of the chancel was an inscription of nine letters of which only five now remain.[8] The first four letters seem to read 'dp(er)ru', and make no obvious sense, a shaded area indicates a break, followed by 'Syr T G', of which only the first letter remains. This must refer to Sir Thomas Golding, Vicar 1489–1529, who was responsible for ensuring that the 'priests service' was established in the 1490s.

In 1501 Sir John Porter, the chantry priest, bequeathed all the money owing to him and arising from the sale of his house, '. . . to make . . . a chapel in the worship of St Mary de Populo within the said churchyard'.[9] This chapel is probably the present vestry, which is a narrower and later addition to the north chapel, built on ground formerly part of the churchyard. Until the 1868 restoration, the vestry had a first-floor room, which may have been the residence of the chantry priest, as at Wingfield.

The parapet of the south chapel has terracotta panels, three of which are lozenges and depict a crowned lion's head, and five are square with a boar surmounted with a crown. The crowned lion's head was one of the badges of Charles Brandon, Lord of the Honour 1514–38, and was used in similar terracotta panels to decorate Westhorpe Hall, and Suffolk Place in London.[10]

The magnificent late 15th-century rood screen has a loft and rood of 1925 designed by Ninian Comper. The screen is reputed to have come from the Great Massingham Priory in Norfolk, although the written 'tradition' dates only from 1922 when Mary Short wrote her 'Historical Reminiscences of Eye'. However, Great Massingham was dissolved in 1475, when the monks joined the community at Westacre. It is possible that Eye then acquired the redundant screen, which has an unexplained extra bay on the north side. One piece of dating evidence is the inscription on one of the vaults 'Pray for John Gold', although no wills have survived for any member of that family at Eye or Massingham. What we do know for certain is that will bequests 1504–16 show a new candlebeam, with the image of Jesus, being painted and gilded. At the Reformation the beam was painted with a text from Matthew 16 v.26 taken from Cranmer's Bible of 1540. 'And Jesus said unto his disciples, what doeth it profet a man yf he wynne all the whole world, and lose his owne soule, or what shall a man geve to redem his soule agayne wythall.'

The church was restored in 1868 by the architect James Colling of London. The evangelical leanings of Sir Edward Clarence Kerrison and the restoration committee, nearly resulted in the rood screen being moved to the arch on the north side of the chancel. Colling managed to persuade the committee to leave the screen,[11] but the candlebeam was moved to the south aisle and has not survived.

The church maintains the Catholic Anglican tradition established by Rev. John Oakey and the Patron, Miss Maud Tacon, in the 1920s.

The Priory of St Peter

The Benedictine Priory of St Peter was founded by Robert Malet probably between the Domesday survey of 1086, when it is not mentioned, and the death of King William in 1087.[1] The Priory was the first Benedictine house to be established in Suffolk after the Conquest and was a cell, or daughter house, of the Abbey of Bernay in Normandy. Eye in turn had a cell at Dunwich.

Robert Malet was deprived of the Lordship of the Honour c.1087 and returned to Normandy until 1100. His successor as Lord, Roger the Poitevin, gave some of Robert's endowment to Charroux in La Marche and the Priory of Lancaster. It therefore seems likely that the Priory at Eye may not have been established, or at least did not enjoy its full endowment, until after 1100. The earliest mention of the monks occurs c.1105. 'Robert the Monk', who may have been in charge before the appointment of a Prior was mentioned c.1109–10 and Hubert the Prior in c.1111–13.[2]

The Priory was richly endowed with the income from 28 churches in Suffolk, Lincolnshire and Norfolk; tithes from 45 parishes; the profit of the three-day St Leonard's fair at Dunwich and the four-day St Peter's fair at Eye. The most important endowment was the tithe of the town of Dunwich, and the income from all the churches that existed or might exist in the town.

The Priory, however, had no saintly shrine, no venerated rood, and no health giving image to attract pilgrims. The sea eroded the income of the Priory as the churches of Dunwich and the small cell fell into the sea, and the area of titheable land was reduced. The nine churches of Dunwich in 1300 had been reduced to four by c.1530. In the same period the income from Dunwich fell from £40 2s 2d in 1291, to £12 13s 4d in 1535.[3] The small cell at Dunwich had fallen into the sea by c.1300. It was probably at this period that the Red Book was brought to the mother house at Eye for safe keeping. Perhaps the seal of Aethelwald, the last Saxon Bishop of Dunwich, was also brought to Eye at the same time.

The site of the Priory was excavated in 1926 and revealed that the church and claustral buildings were an exact replica of the Priory in Bernay. The Priory church lay to the south-east of the present house, within the area bounded by the crinkle-crankle wall and the curving hedge.[4] A series of fish ponds and stews survive to the north of Abbey Farm, which served as the Priory fish-farm.

The Abbot of Bernay appointed the Prior of Eye, and therefore the Priory was regarded as an alien institution. This led to the continual impoverishment of the Priory, as the Crown confiscated most of the revenue whenever England and France were at war. During the Hundred Years War the income declined from £160 in 1337 to only £20 in 1379. In the latter year the church, cloister, refectory and all the other possessions of the Priory were described as '. . . feeble and ruinous' and could not be repaired for less than 1,000 marks (£666 13s 4d).[5] The number of monks never exceeded 10, but in 1379 the income could support only the Prior and 3 monks.

In 1385 Queen Ann, consort of Richard II and Lord of the Honour of Eye, arranged for the Priory to come under English patronage. All the debts were forgiven and '. . . certain persons at great expense intend of their alms to relieve and repair the Priory'.[6] Part of the Prior's lodging was rebuilt after 1385 and some of the structure is preserved as part of Abbey Farm. The present house is a tall 17th-century building faced with red brick. The side or east wall of the house is the west wall of the Priory cloister. The timber-framed rear or north wing was part of the Prior's lodging, and a south-facing traceried window of timber still survives within the house.

The Valor Ecclesiasticus of 1535 shows the total income from churches and land to be £184 9s 7½d. The regular annual expenditure was £23 17s 4½d, including £6 1s 8d paid at the rate of 4d a day on bread for six poor people; £1 6s 8d in bread for the poor, and £6 13s 4d to feed and clothe 'four poor boys who serve in the church'.[7]

In October 1534 the Prior, Sub Prior and six monks signed the Oath of Supremacy. On 26 August 1536 an Inventory and Valuation was made of the Priory by the King's Commissioners, which showed it to have been in a very impoverished state, many items being described as 'old' or 'lytell or nothyng worth'. Amongst the items in the Vestry were '3 lytell boxes of sylver with relyques' worth 11s 8d; 'an arme of tymber garnysshed with sylver, called Saint Blasis arm,' 5s; and an 'olde Masse boke called the redde boke of Eye garnysshed with

Seal of the Priory of St Peter

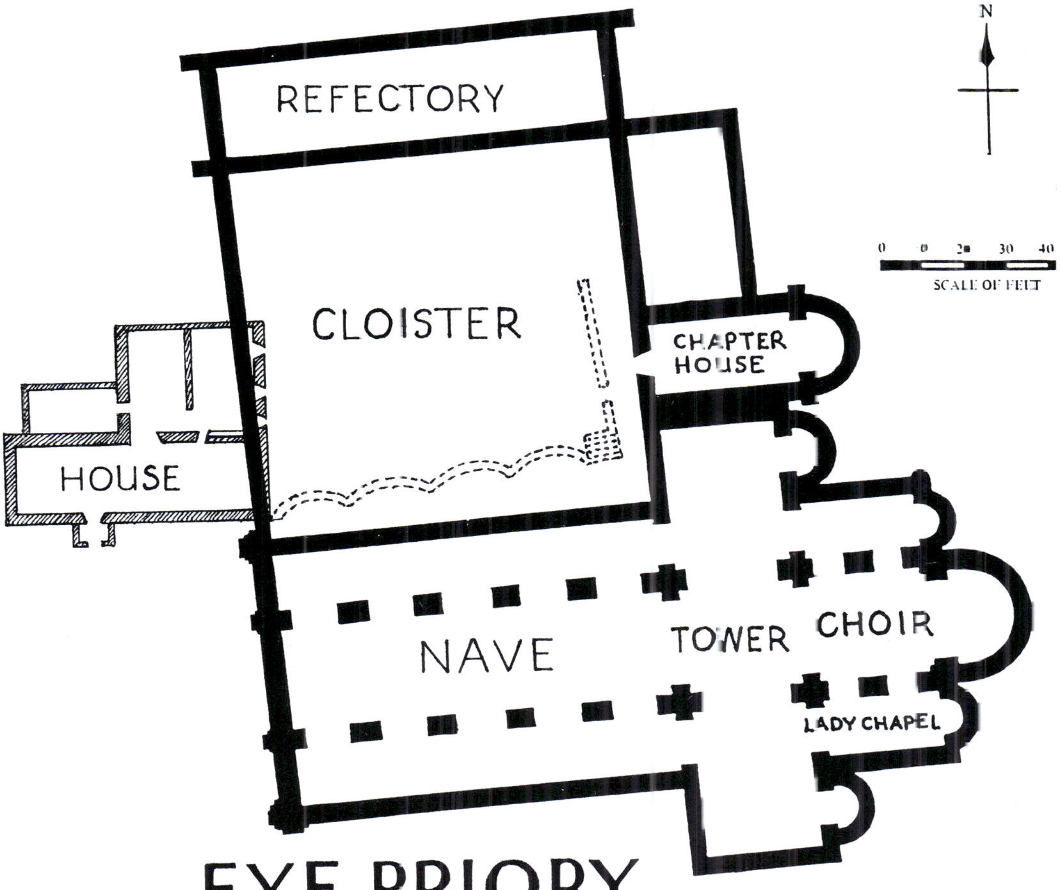

EYE PRIORY

a lytell sylver on the one side, the residewe lytell worth, 20d'. The total value of the contents came to £29 11s 2d, with a further £16 6s 8d in corn and livestock.[8]

The Priory was suppressed on 12 February 1537, and the 10-acre site granted on 7 April 1537, to Charles Brandon, Duke of Suffolk and Lord of the Honour of Eye. William Parker the last Prior was granted a pension of £18 a year.

The red brick building to the west of Abbey Farm has been described as both a chapel, and a guesthouse. However, there is no evidence for a chapel so close to the Priory church, or to explain why a guesthouse should be so much grander than the Prior's own lodgings. The building dates from c.1500, was originally two storeyed, and has a fine range of single and double light windows and a central doorway on the west side.

Although much of the interior was damaged by a fire, described as occurring 'some years ago' in 1927, there is evidence of a superior chamber on the first floor at the southern end, with stone mullioned windows and a niche.[9]

This imposing structure, with high quality brickwork, is most likely to have been the residence of the Steward of the Honour of Eye. The castle complex would have been reduced to ruins and a prison by 1500, and a site near the Priory would have made a fitting administrative centre. Charles Brandon certainly dated many of his letters from Eye[10] and probably used the building during visits to the headquarters of the Honour. It is interesting to note that one of the chambers in the Prior's lodging was called the 'Queen's Chamber' after Princess Mary Tudor, Dowager Queen of France and wife of Charles Brandon.

There was also a Gatehouse described as being 'near the road to the south of the Priory'. The foundations were still visible in 1862, but had been removed by 1881 when the Ordnance Survey map was drawn up. The office of Porter became hereditary in 1255, when, in exchange for guarding the Priory Gate and going on the Prior's business anywhere in England, he was to receive the diet of a servant eating with the household; a horse and stabling; a chicken at Christmas for every 20 brought into the Priory; and 3 oxen at Easter for every 100 brought into the Priory.[11]

Brick building at the Priory of c.1500. This photograph of c.1910 shows stone mullioned windows in the end and side walls, which were destroyed by fire before 1927.

The Red Book of Eye

The Red Book was a copy of the Gospels, supposed to have belonged to St Felix, which derived its name from the colour of the leather cover. St Felix established the See of East Anglia at Dunwich c.632. As we saw earlier, Eye Priory was granted all the churches of Dunwich as part of its foundation endowment, and the daughter cell of Eye at Dunwich had been abandoned by c.1300.

Sometime between 1534 and 1537 John Leyland visited Eye Priory and recorded that, '. . . the monks of Eye still preserve a Book of the Gospels, a relic of their ruined cell. It is popularly called the Red Book of Eye, and the people are wont to swear by it. The monks constantly affirm that it was Felix's book; and certainly that seems likely enough, for besides the fact that it is written in large Lombardic letters, it has the appearance of wonderful great antiquity'.[1]

The Red Book was still at the Priory in August 1536, when it was recorded in the inventory. The fate of the book after the suppression of the Priory in early 1537 is uncertain. Bishop Tanner in the 18th century thought it was in Archbishop Matthew Parker's collection in Corpus Christi College Library, but M. R. James in 1899 disputed that the book in question had come from Eye.[2] It is, however, probable that part of the book has survived amongst the Egerton manuscripts in the British library.[3]

In the 19th and 20th centuries, there was the lingering hope that the Red Book might be among the Borough archives at the Town Hall. However, in October 1843 Thomas French, a solicitor and antiquarian of Eye wrote '. . . though I have several times had occasion to examine the records of the Borough, I have never been able to discover this book or anything regarding its disappearance'.[4] An enduring story is that the parchment was cut up in the 19th century to make game tickets at Brome Hall! However, the Priory would have had more than one medieval manuscript amongst its archives. It is possible that one of these also had a red cover, and may have been vandalised at Brome Hall. If only one of the game tickets could be located and identified, we would be a little nearer a solution to the problem.

The Seal of Aethelwald

The seal of Aethelwald, the last Saxon Bishop of the See of East Anglia at Dunwich c.845–69, may have been brought to Eye by the Dunwich monks c.1300. The seal was discovered c.1820 in a garden 200 yards from the Priory, by a labourer whose child threw it into a fire, and whose wife rescued it again.[1]

The seal is now in the British Museum. It is of bronze, mitre shaped, with three tiers of arches surmounted by a fleur-de-lis, and has nine wolves' heads in the intersections of the arches. The eyes were originally formed with small garnets, only one of which survives.

Eye Park

The park at Eye was one of only four recorded in the Suffolk Domesday Book, and had been established by either William or Robert Malet 1066–86. The open area of park used for hunting lay to the south of the castle and the low lying moor, and was reached by a causeway.

The park was enclosed with a fence by Henry, Duke of Louvaine and Brabant, Lord of the Honour, sometime between 1198 and 1205. As part of their obligation as tenants, several manors in the Honour were made responsible for the repair of the park paling and the causeway, which may have been the present Park Lane.

In 1313 thieves broke into the 'King's Park at Eye' and drove away cattle, which resulted in an investigation into the state of the paling around the park.[1] The inquisition, or investigation, showed that 'beyond the memory of man' the tenants in Brundish, Tannington, Badingham, Dennington, Laxfield, Stradbroke, Kenton and Eye, had been '. . . bound to repair the paling about the park of the King's Honour of Eye, and the causeway to the town of Eye'. The new timber and oak were always provided by the Bailiff of the Honour, and the tenants were allowed to take any felled timber unfit for paling for their own use. From the details of the inquisition it appears that the tenants were responsible for repairing 1,842 yards of the park paling and 185 yards of the causeway.[2] Unfortunately these figures are of no help in calculating the size of the park or the length of the causeway, as the unknown remainder of the paling and causeway was repaired by the Lord of the Honour.

There are very few details of the subsequent history of the park. In 1329 Edward III ordered all the deer, bucks and does to be brought from the park at Hoxne, presumably belonging to the Bishop of Norwich, and taken to Eye Park.[3]

The custom of the tenants taking away the tops of trees, felled to repair the palings of Eye Park, was mentioned in a letter of July 1578 from the Deputy Surveyor of the Queen's Parks to Lord Burghley.[4] In 1591 a Special Commission examined the state of the '. . . pales and dytches' around the Park, and discovered that the various parishes had not been maintaining the pales, with the result that '. . . a great part of the pale about the said park was broken down'.[5]

Unfortunately we do not know what measures were taken as a result of the Commission, but the Park had passed into private hands by at least 1654. In that year William Small, of Swanton Morley in Norfolk, bequeathed an annual rent charge of £10, for apprenticing male children of Eye, from his 'Messuage and lands called Eye Park'.[6] Some of the land may have remained as park or extensive pleasure grounds as Ralph Adams, who was buried at Brome in 1775, was described as '. . . of Eye Parkeeper'.[7]

The present Eye Park House is probably on the site of the former keeper's lodge, roughly in the centre of the Park, near the River Dove.

Seal of Aethelwald, Bishop of East Anglia c.845–69.

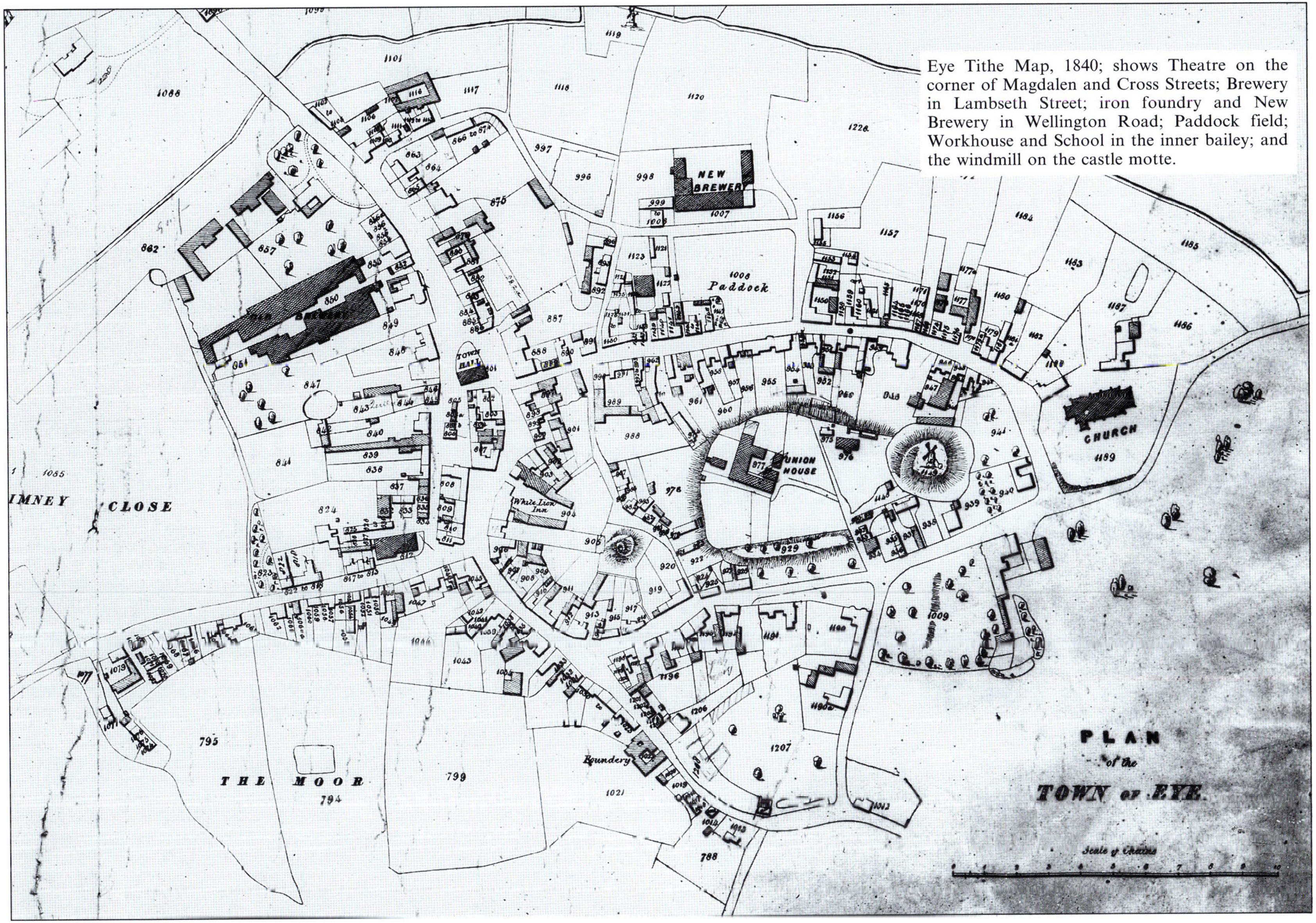

Eye Tithe Map, 1840; shows Theatre on the corner of Magdalen and Cross Streets; Brewery in Lambseth Street; iron foundry and New Brewery in Wellington Road; Paddock field; Workhouse and School in the inner bailey; and the windmill on the castle motte.

Charter and Borough

In 1575 Eye obtained a new charter from Queen Elizabeth I. This confirmed all the earlier charters dating back to one of King John in 1205, which was 203 years before Eye actually received its first charter.

In the late 19th century it became obvious that both Eye, often spelt Eia, and Hythe in Kent, often spelt Heya, claimed the 1205 charter as the origin of their borough status. The charter granted privileges of trade and shipwreck that could only belong to a coastal town. The meeting place mentioned was called 'Shippewaya', an open space in Hythe, and not the 'Town house called the Toll House' in which the burgesses of Eye met. This problem was neatly explained in the 1566 Constitution by describing the meeting place as the '. . . town house of old time called Sypweia, now named the Toll House'.[1] Both the 1575 Charter and 1579 Constitutions refer to the 'common hall called Syppewaye'.[2] In all three documents Eye is described as 'Eye otherwise Heya'.

In 1885 the Town Clerk of Hythe drew attention to the joint claims to the early charter, and proved that it belonged to Hythe. In 1955, Philip Dickinson made the same point again whilst lecturing in Eye, and caused the abandonment of the 750th celebration of the charter. In 1959 Derek Charman, joint archivist of Ipswich and East Suffolk, and his assistant Jean Imray, who catalogued the Eye borough archives, finally resolved the confusion.[3]

Eye became a borough between 1066 and 1071 when William Malet built his castle, and established a market, which had 25 burgesses or freemen by 1086. Eye was a 'mense' or signeurial borough, gaining its status as the headquarters of the Honour, and holding its privileges from the Lord of the Honour, and not from the King. The town of Eye was not specifically mentioned until 1337, and was subsumed in the phrase 'the castle, manor and Honour of Eye'. However, the 1337 grant of the Honour, by Edward III to Robert Ufford, Earl of Suffolk, gives the first mention of 'the castle, town, manor and Honour of Eye'.[4]

Eye received its first charter on 29 January 1408 from King Henry IV which was preceded by Letters Patent confirming the 1205 charter of King John, which had actually been granted to Hythe. The confusion may possibly have come from the spelling of Eye and Hythe, mistaken by an official of the Honour or Priory, when searching for ancient grants amongst the rolls of the Court of Chancery in London.

The charter of 1408, in common with many others of the period, contained a 'clause licet' which empowered the recipients to exercise the rights contained in the original grant, even though there was no evidence of their ever having done so in the past. The 1408 grant is the first charter of the Borough of Eye, and an early 15th-century copy was included amongst the Priory archives.[5] The earliest reference to the two Bailiffs of Eye occurs in 1420, when Richard Hull and John Glover, held a Court for the Borough of Eye.[6] In 1453–54 the Chamberlains paid 2s 11d '. . . for making le mase at Norwich'.

A deed of 1457, by which the 'Bailiffs and Commonality of Eye' granted land to John Sulyard, has the earliest surviving borough seal.[7] This shows that the townsmen were exercising two of the most important rights of a chartered borough, that of using a common seal, of holding land, and implies a third, that of perpetual succession. Townsmen left land to the Bailiffs for the benefit of the whole community. For example, in 1479 Robert Anyell bequeathed 'Fodysmere meadow by the Kynges Brygge' to pay the 'common fine', and all his market stalls towards the support of the Bailiffs.[8]

In 1480 the Lord of the Honour, John de la Pole Duke of Suffolk, made the important grant of abolishing the annual payment of £4 for the 'farm of the market'.[9] The Bailiffs and Burgesses of the Town and Borough of Eye were from henceforth responsible for regulating and profiting from the traders in the market.

The 1205 and 1408 charters were confirmed and renewed in the usual way, by each successive monarch in 1414; 1425; 1461, 1491, when the Chamberlains paid 15s 8d for the 'renewal of the charter'; 1510; and 1551 when the Chamberlains paid £5 6s 8d for the renewal, and 19s 10d '. . . allowed to Robert London for riding to London to renew the charter'.[10]

On 31 August 1559 '. . . there went certain men of Eye to Redgrave, to see my Lord Keeper of the Great Seal, to speak with his Lordship, concerning their town land, and diveres other matters within the town . . .' which must have included the town charter. Two of the townsmen returned to Sir Nicholas Bacon on 4 September, and collected Letters Patent of Inspeximus and Confirmation of the charter, dated 2 September 1559. The cost of the confirmation was £4 15s which included '. . . £1 4d for the Confirmation of the Seal; 10s for the fynne; £2 6s 8d for the wryting and enrollment; 10s for a veloine skynne drawing and florishyng; 3s for wax and lace; and 4s for the examination.'[11] The charter was finally confirmed in April 1560. This activity does not mean that Queen Elizabeth was at Redgrave in 1559, but rather that Sir Nicholas, as Lord Keeper, had the legal and administrative authority to grant such a confirmation. Sir Nicholas also granted a confirmation of the charter of Dunwich on 21 September 1559, whilst at Redgrave.[12]

At least three sets of Constitutions for the Borough were drawn up in the 16th century. These bye-laws regulated the Bailiffs, Burgesses, Freemen, Officials, inhabitants, market, town moor, Grammar School and borough charities. In 1547–8 the Chamberlains paid 4d for the '. . . wryting off the boke of constytucyons'.[13] Disputes and disagreements resulted in a legal suit at the Court of Star Chamber in 1566. A new set of constitutions was drawn up by the Bailiffs and Burgesses, at the direction of the Duke of Norfolk, in September 1566, which was in turn replaced by the Constitutions of September 1579.[14]

A new charter was granted by Queen Elizabeth in 1575 which included all the Hythe privileges mentioned above, and with the 1579 Constitutions became the governing instruments of the Borough until 1697.

The members of the Corporation '. . . being wholly ignorant of the law . . . neglected to subscribe' to the 1695 'Act for the better securing of his Majesties Royal Person and Government'. As a result the Corporation was made '. . . unfitt and uncapable to bear or exercise their respective offices . . . and the body corporate . . . for want of fit members languished . . .'.[15] The Elizabethan charter was null and void, and the Borough without legal government. A new charter was granted by William III in October 1697, based on that of 1575, which remained in force until the Municipal Corporations Act of 1835.

Until 1835 Eye was governed by two Bailiffs, who were also Magistrates and Clerks of the Market for their year in office, 10 Principal and 24 Common Burgesses, a Recorder and a Coroner. Other borough officials were the two Sergeants at Mace; two Chamberlains, who managed the town moor; two Constables who also collected rates and taxes; two Alefounders, to check the quality and measures of bread and beer in the Borough; and a Gaoler.

The Corporation was a self-perpetuating oligarchy. The two Bailiffs were elected each year by and from the 12 Principal Burgesses; when a Principal Burgess died a replacement was elected from the 24 Common Burgesses by the 12 Principal Burgesses; and new Common Burgesses were elected by the 24 from amongst the Freemen.

After 1835 the Corporation comprised a Mayor, 4 Aldermen and 12 Councillors, with a Town Clerk, Treasurer, Town Crier, two Sergeants at Mace and two Chamberlains. As the responsibilities of the Council increased, so the borough officials were appointed to manage housing, rates, public health and other areas.

The Borough received a Grant of Arms from Queen Elizabeth on 20 April 1592. The grant or Patent was made by the Garter King of Arms, who had been '. . . influenced by the consideration of the ancient grants, and by the persuasion of certain noble and high born men (including Sir Thomas Cornwallis of Brome, Sir Nicholas Bacon of Redgrave, son of the Lord Keeper, and Edward Grimston of Rishangles, M.P. for Eye) and also by the request of the Bailiffs, Burgesses and Commonality of the Manor and Burgh of Eye'.[16] The Borough accounts for 1591–2 show payments of £3 3s 4d for '. . . the Patent of the Arms of the Town, to the King of Herehalts (Heralds)' and 6s 6d '. . . to the wryter of the Patent and for his seal'.[17]

The shield has a cross and four martlets from the arms of Edward the Confessor, and an eagle with outstretched wings supported by two sprays of roses derived from the royal emblems of Queen Elizabeth. The crest has a helmet and mantle with the Crown of the Imperial Sun, surmounted by the 16-pointed Star of Innocence, with the all seeing eye of God in the centre. The motto 'Occulus in Coelum' means 'Eye to Heaven'. The most recent renewal of the Arms was in 1952 by Queen Elizabeth II.

In 1992 the town celebrated the 400th anniversary of the granting of the Arms with the Mayor's Ball, an exhibition of archives, a lecture, and by presenting commemorative mugs to all the Primary School pupils. After 566 years as a chartered borough, Eye lost that status, as a result of Local Government reorganisation, in 1974. Eye, which had the distinction of being the second oldest chartered borough in Suffolk, and the smallest borough in the United Kingdom, now became a parish within Mid-Suffolk District Council. The ancient Court Leet, by which the Bailiffs had regulated the highways, and the Court of Pie Poudre, by which they had settled disputes at fairs were also abolished in 1974.

However, historic links are still retained; the parish council retained the name 'Eye Town Council'; the chairman is known as the Mayor and still wears robes and chain, the latter presented by Charles Tacon, of White House Lambseth Street, in 1901; the Mayor, Town Clerk and Macebearer, all in traditional dress, still process to church, accompanied by the town councillors and representatives of local organisations, on the annual Mayor's Sunday in May, and Remembrance Sunday; the Borough Regalia, including two small 16th-century maces are still in use; the Town Council still meets in the Council Chamber at the Town Hall; and in 1976 the Borough Arms were regranted to the new Town Council.[18]

Mayor's Sunday 1909/10. Col. James Wilkins, Mayor; Harold Warnes, Town clerk; Mr William Short (with beard) on extreme right.

Roads in the Borough

The Bailiffs had responsibility, through the Court Leet, for keeping the streets clean and free from obstructions. For example in 1593 Thomas Carter, a grocer, was fined for '. . . that he annoyeth the heighe streetes with filth and myer by him shoveled up and there remayninge', and Andrew Haweys for '. . . that the watercourse which runneth against his house in the street, is a common annusance, and is henceforth to be kept sweete and cleane'.[1] Fines were also imposed for leaving dunghills or timber in the street, allowing hogs to run free, overflowing gutters and throwing 'water' out of doors or windows into the street.[2]

In 1879 it was proposed that the footpaths should be 'paved'. Until then it seems that individual house holders, shops and businesses had maintained the path outside their premises. Between 1890 and 1896 tar paths were laid in Magdalen, Church and Castle Streets.[3]

Until the roads were sealed a water cart, supplied from a pump at Lambseth Bridge, used to sprinkle the streets to lay the dust. As Charles Etheridge recalled '. . . there were no tar roads; the street and other roads were made of granite stones which were put down in the winter and rolled in. The streets were very rough and dusty, and wore boots and shoes out quickly'.[4]

Castle Street c.1880. The shop on the left is Gillings, watch and clock maker, who seems to have ceased trading 1883/5. Anthony Scoulding Gissing, baker and grocers shop is on the right, and the baker's ovens are still in situ in the basement.

The Town Moor

As we have seen, Eye is surrounded on three sides by low lying land, that is liable to flood. Part of this land, amounting to about 23 acres, to the south of Magdalen Street was the Town Moor, owned by the Corporation and managed by two Chamberlains appointed each year. The land is now used for a Playing Field, Community Centre, and a nature reserve.

The Chamberlains' Accounts have survived, with many gaps, from 1410 to 1620. These show that income was derived from the annual sale of 10 acres of grass, and the charges made for grazing rights for the Freemen's horses and cattle, known as agistment, comprised the main income of the Borough until the 17th century.

The Chamberlains were also the Borough Treasurers until the mid 17th century, when a new post of Treasurer was created. The income from the Moor was spent in repairing Borough property such as the Tollhouse, Gaol, Workhouse, Market Cross and cleaning the Market Place each week. Money was spent on maintaining the hedges, fences, ditches and bridges of the Moor, providing a rook net for the town, and a secure ring to tether the bull.

Another important function was to provide and maintain the Town Butts, or targets for archery practice. By an Act of Parliament in 1477 every man had to practise archery weekly, as part of the local Militia training. The Butts were situated at the south-west corner of the Moor, just to the north of Moor Hall, in a small enclosure with banks on three sides. In the late 19th century the Butts were used as targets in the rifle range of the Eye Rifle Volunteers.

The Borough Constitutions of 1566 and 1578 gave Freemen having less than 10 acres of land, the right to pasture two cows and a horse on the Moor, paying 2s 8d for each cow and 4s for the horse. With the abolition of Freemen under the 1832 Reform Act, the number entitled to use the Moor steadily declined as the existing Freemen died. The Borough Council then let the 'goings on the Moor' either by tender, or for a fixed rental. The First Moor, now the nature reserve, continued to be let until the 1970s, and the Second Moor, now the Playing Field, until the First World War.

In 1921, permission was granted by the Council for part of the Second Moor to be used for cricket and football. Following the Silver Jubilee of King George V in 1935, this part of the Moor became a children's playground with play equipment.[1] The Eye Playing Field Association leased 6 acres of the Moor in 1957, and in 1962 a playing field was made adjacent to Magdalen Street. At about this time the Borough Council planted several acres with willow and poplar as a cash crop.

In 1967 Eye Community Council was formed, and the following year purchased 8 acres of the Moor for a nominal sum, and also the remaining 14 acres of the First Moor in 1974. A building used as a pavilion and changing rooms was erected in 1973.[2] In 1981 the Community Council decided to open up the plantation to walkers and sold half the mature poplars to finance the project. Most of the willows were felled because they were diseased. The following year oak, ash, alder, birch and other broadleaved trees were planted, largely funded by personal subscription in Eye.

The gale of October 1987 snapped off a large proportion of the poplar trees, and gave impetus to the efforts, begun in 1982, to transform the 14 acres of the First Moor, part of which had been the Borough rubbish dump, into a nature reserve featuring environmental art. The area has been planted with 32 species of native trees; with roses, clematis and honeysuckle and contains stacks of branches for wildlife habitats. Other features include an enormous osier circle of rings of differently coloured willow; a maze; the south pond with a viewing hill; the Dragonfly Pond over which is suspended a giant dragonfly; a moat; numerous paths, bridges, seats, clearings and two carved thrones. The project was supported by local councils and voluntary groups.

In 1990 the Chugai Boyeki Corporation of Tokyo, through their links with Life Science Research (now Pharmaco-L.S.R.) of Occold, donated £1,000 to the Eye Town Moors Trust (now Woodland Society) as a symbol of trust and friendship between the peoples of Japan and England. The money was used to help create the 'Pond of the Rising Sun'.[3]

The Community Council dissolved itself in 1990, and handed over its funds to the new Playing Field Association who were co-ordinating the provision of a Community Centre which was opened in September 1991.[4]

Elections and Patronal Families

In April 1571 Eye was enfranchised and able to send two Burgesses, or M.P.s, to Parliament. The townsmen of Eye regarded Sir Nicholas Bacon of Redgrave, Lord Keeper of the Great Seal, and Steward of the Honour of Eye, as their patron. There is little doubt that the enfranchisement was due to Bacon's influence at Court, and he had been active in settling the Borough's affairs since at least 1559.[1] The Bacon family regarded Eye as a 'pocket borough' and a safe seat for their own nominees. Thus from the onset of Parliamentary representation, the seat was dominated by the local influential family. The Bacons of Redgrave controlled Borough elections from 1571 until the mid-17th century.

The electorate of Eye was limited to freemen, and those inhabitants paying 'scot and lot' (land taxes). The number of electors, including the 36 members of the Corporation, stood at between 150 and 180 until the 1832 Reform Act.

The Cornwallis family had been resident at Brome since the early 15th century, and were related to the Bacons, by the marriage in 1614 of Nathaniel Bacon and Jane, widow of Sir William Cornwallis. The Bacon estates centred on Redgrave and Culford, and those of Cornwallis at Brome eventually descended to Sir Frederick Cornwallis, who had become M.P. for Eye in 1640.

From 1640–1820, the Cornwallis family usually nominated themselves, their relations, or friends as candidates for election. Although Eye was a pocket borough it required careful nursing, and Lord Cornwallis, when at Brome, had to be ever attentive to the needs of the Borough. There were several contested elections in the 17th century, but only one in the 18th century. This occurred in 1747 when John Cornwallis voted against his brother's interest in Parliament. Lord Cornwallis would not re-nominate John, and instead chose his brother-in-law Roger Townsend as the member.

In 1823 Charles 2nd (and last) Marquis Cornwallis died and was buried at Culford. The estates around Eye were purchased by Matthias Kerrison of Bungay, for his son General Sir Edward Kerrison.

The Kerrisons of Oakley Park in Hoxne continued the political dominance of the seat by one family. Sir Edward was elected unopposed in 1824 and remained one of the M.P.s until the 1832 Reform Act. In 1830 William Cobbett visited Eye, and described it as '. . . a beautiful little place, though an exceedingly rotten Borough'.[2]

By the 1832 Act Eye lost one of its M.P.s, and the electoral area was extended from the Borough to include the 10 surrounding parishes. Sir Edward remained the unopposed member until his death in 1853. The seat then passed to his son Sir Edward Clarence Kerrison, who held it unopposed until 1866, when he resigned to become M.P. for East Suffolk.

Such was the close link between the Kerrisons and their 'electorate', that when Sir Edward Clarence became engaged the local newspaper inserted the following: '. . . It is generally reported that a young gentleman who one day may inherit a large estate, including a snug little borough, is about turning Whig, that he has fixed his affections upon a lady, the daughter of the Earl of Ilchester, whose family are of the same politics. It is also said the tailors in the borough are looking forward for a good job – many coats, to the tune of one or two hundred, it is anticipated will have to be turned with new trimmings'.[3]

In 1885 the Borough of Eye became part of the new larger North-East or Eye Division of Suffolk. In 1918, and again in 1948, the area was further extended and called the Eye Constituency. At a further reorganisation in 1983, the area was divided between St Edmundsbury, Central Suffolk and Suffolk Coastal.[4]

Since 1866, when Eye ceased to be a 'pocket borough', the constituency returned a Liberal member 1885–1923 and 1929–51, and a Conservative 1866–85, 1923–9 and 1951 to the present (1993). The longest serving members this century have been Edgar Granville, later Lord Granville of Eye, 1929–51, and Sir Michael Harwood Harrison 1951–79. Since its creation in 1983 the Central Suffolk Constituency has been represented by Michael Lord.

The Cornwallis Family

The Cornwallis family had lived at the manor of Ling Hall in Brome since c.1410. Sir Thomas Cornwallis (1519–1604) Privy Councillor, Treasurer of Calais and Comptroller of the Household under Queen Mary, acquired the Manor of Brome Hall c.1550, and built a new Hall there c.1560. The family had been active in the affairs of Eye since at least 1495, when John Cornwallis granted a licence to the Grammar School.

The first Cornwallis to serve as M.P. for Eye was Sir Frederick (1611–62) who represented the Borough 1640–42. He was also the Steward of the Honour of Eye 1639–49 and 1660–62. Sir Frederick supported the King in the Civil War, was with him at Oxford, fought in the Battle of Cropredy in Oxfordshire in 1644, and went into exile with Charles II. At the Restoration in 1660 he was created Baron Cornwallis of Eye.

Charles, 2nd Lord Cornwallis (1632–73) was M.P. for Eye 1660–62, and Steward of the Honour 1671–3. Charles, 4th Lord Cornwallis (1675-1721) was M.P. for Eye 1695–8, and in 1698 obtained the grant of the Honour of Eye from William III. Charles, 5th Lord Cornwallis (1701–62) was a Courtier, held the office of Groom of the Bedchamber, and was created Viscount Brome and Earl Cornwallis in 1753. Culford Hall near Bury St. Edmunds was now the main family seat. A letter of 1752 mentions 'As Culford is the favourite, nothing is being done here (Brome) but just preserving the house from wind and weather'.[1]

General Charles Cornwallis (1738–1805) the 2nd Earl was created Marquis Cornwallis in 1792 for his services in America and India. Like all his predecessors he was M.P. for Eye 1760–72 until he succeeded to the family titles. He took a leading role in the War of Independence 1776–82, and his surrender of Yorktown marked the end of the war. He was Governor General of India in 1786–93 and 1805, and Lord Lieutenant of Ireland 1798–1801.

Charles, 2nd and last Marquis (1774–1823) was M.P. for Eye in 1795. On his death the estates around Eye were purchased by Matthias Kerrison of Bungay.

Sir Edward Clarence Kerrison (1821–86).

The Kerrison and Bateman-Hanbury Families

In 1817 Matthias Kerrison of Bungay purchased the Hoxne Hall Estate from Lord Maynard, and in 1825 the former Cornwallis estates in Brome, Oakley, Denham, Eye and several neighbouring parishes.

The estate inherited by General Sir Edward Kerrison amounted to nearly 10,000 acres. In percentage terms this included 85% of the land in Oakley, 83% of Denham, 62% of Eye, 55% of Brome, 47% of Hoxne and 22% of Yaxley.[1] In 1830 Sir Edward rebuilt Hoxne Hall to the designs of Sidney Smirke, who also designed the famous circular Reading Room at the British Museum. The mansion was renamed Oakley Park, and became the seat of the Kerrison family. Sir Edward had fought throughout the Peninsular War from 1808 to 1814, retired from active service after Waterloo, and was created a Baronet in 1821. General Sir Edward Kerrison G.C.H., Colonel of the 14th Dragoons, and unopposed M.P. for Eye since 1824, died in March 1853 aged 79 years.

Sir Edward Clarence Kerrison (1821–86) the second and last Baronet, was the unopposed M.P. for Eye 1853–66, and for East Suffolk 1866–7. He was described in 1875 as '. . . having planned more institutions, organisations and public works than any other man in Suffolk during the last quarter century'.[2] He advocated the cultivation of flax in the district and built a flax works at Eye in 1851 and 1864; built Thorndon Reformatory, which was later called the Kerrison School, in 1856; promoted and paid nearly half the cost of the new Town Hall in 1857; promoted and became a director of the Mellis and Eye railway in 1864, built and equipped the Working Men's Hall and Reading Room in Lambseth Street in 1867, was the principal subscriber to the restoration of Eye Church in 1868; founded the Eye Medical Club in 1876 which eventually had over 2,000 members; was the chairman of the Hartismere Board of Guardians; a Governor of Eye Grammar School, and a major subscriber to Eye National School.

The gothic style memorial in Broad Street was designed in 1888 by James Colling of London, whom Sir Edward had employed to restore the Church and Guildhall, and to design the National School on Castle Hill. The four coats of arms are Kerrison impaling Fox-Strangewayes (the family of Lady Caroline Kerrison), Eye, Kerrison and the Suffolk Regiment.

The estate passed to Sir Edward's sister Agnes who had married Lord Bateman of Shobdon in Herefordshire. After her husband's death in 1901, Lady Bateman lived at Brome Hall with some of her unmarried children. She died in March 1918 and was buried at Shobdon. A memorial was erected to her in Oakley church by her daughter Agnes Rosamund Bateman-Hanbury, who also presented a portrait to the Town Council.

Following Lady Bateman's death the estate was broken up. The 'Brome Hall estate' amounting to nearly 3,000 acres, including Eye Park and Abbey Farm, was first offered for sale in May 1921.[3] Oakley Park with 1,300 acres had been sold prior to 1921, and the hall was demolished in 1930.

Miss Maud Tacon, daughter of Sir Thomas Tacon of Red House, purchased Brome Hall with 400 acres, which were in turn sold in several lots, following her death in October 1952.[4] Brome Hall was demolished in 1958.[5]

The Market Place

As we have seen earlier, between 1066 and 1071 William Malet established a Saturday market, with 25 burgesses at Eye. The Domesday entry for Hoxne records that the new market at Eye was held on the same day as the Bishop of East Anglia's market at Hoxne. Trade at Eye market, helped by the presence of the castle as the administrative headquarters of the Honour, grew rapidly and eclipsed Hoxne. 'The Bishop's market has been so far spoilt, that it is of little worth, and now it is set up on Fridays.'[1]

The market place was the large rectangular area, to the west of the entrance to the outer bailey, bounded today by Broad Street and Cross Street. As in most market places, however, later buildings have been built on the open area. The three irregular blocks of buildings, around the site of the Market Cross, developed from stall sites which became permanent shops, the butcher's shambles and dwellings. For example as late as 1725, Stephen Gissing a yeoman of Eye bequeathed '. . . my two Butchers' Stalls or Shambles, now converted into a shopp . . . in the Butchery of Eye'.[2]

The Market Cross stood in the open square between Cross House and 8A The Cross, where the street name 'The Cross' is fixed. In 1839 the square and the road leading to the Town Hall, were called 'Taper Bit Square'.[3]

There is very little evidence, apart from the occasional payment for repairs, relating to the Market Cross. For example in 1542 the Chamberlains paid 1s 8d for 'ledying of the cross for 5 days work', and 2s for making the 'fane of the cross'.[4] In 1582 they spent £1 on timber work 'about the cross and pillorye',[5] and in 1589 paid £1 13s 1d for timber, boards, bricks, lime and clay to seal the joists of the 'cross in the market place'.[6]

The only illustration of the Cross comes from Miss Mary Short's 'Historical Reminiscences of Eye.' The other two drawings in the book are taken from a photograph and an engraving, and we must assume she had access to an original from which she made her drawing. The Cross is shown as a ten-sided wooden, one storey structure, with a brick base, tiled roof and weather vane. The side towards Cross House is open, but all the others appear to be glazed, which is certainly unusual and may be artistic licence. Similar open-sided market crosses can still be seen at Mildenhall, Bungay and Swaffham.

The Cross was demolished after September 1838, in order that the square could be used for the Cattle Market. The Cross was described as being '. . . very ancient and unsightly and consequently as regards the repairs and size thereof a continual charge upon the Borough fund. The said building was originally designed for a market cross, but it has been for a long time discontinued for such purpose, and has become a receptacle for, and the inhabitants in its vicinity consider it, a nuisance.'[7] The building had gone by 1839 when it was not marked on the Tithe Map.

The site of the Town Hall is another encroachment, on which formerly stood the Toll House, Gaol, Workhouse, and a building for the freemen. The Toll House probably derived its name from its function as the place for paying market dues and tolls, and keeping the standard weights and measures. In 1653 the Bailiffs purchased a 14lb and a 28lb iron weight; a set of 10 brass avoirdupois weights, including 1, 2 and 4lb; a pair of 'schales for bread weights;' and a 'yard wand'[8]

The Bailiffs granted leases for stall sites, recorded sales of livestock, maintained standard weights and measures, and regulated the trading and organisation of the market. The 1579 Constitutions forbade horses to be tethered outside houses in the market place; all the stalls and trestles were to be removed each Saturday night; 'no muckhills or lothsome annoyances caused by slaughter of beastes . . .' and the resulting 'corrupt savors' were not to remain in the market, but had to be removed out of the town and buried. Any trader in Eye who sold '. . . grayne, fruit or vyctualls' in any other market had to sell goods of the same quality at every market held in Eye.[9]

The Bailiffs held Courts as Clerks of the Market. For example in 1675 John Clarke, a shopkeeper, was fined 6s 8d for using '. . . unlawful reeles for the measuring of his thread . . . that the thread doth want of its length'; 6s 8d because the thread '. . . doth want 6 and some 8 threads in every skaine'; and 5s because he '. . . keepeth a reele to buy by and others that are false to sell by'. At the same Court seven others were fined for '. . . unlawful bushells and half pecks', and four others for using unlawful weights.[10]

The market was held on a Saturday from 1066–71 until c.1824–9; on a Tuesday until c.1865–8; and then on a Monday until the present day. After the opening of the railway in 1867, a separate livestock market was held near the station. The auctions, which were first mentioned in the 1883 Directory, were held fortnightly by Bonds of Ipswich until c.1930, and then weekly by Moore, Garrard and Son of Hoxne.

The Town Hall, rebuilt in 1757 and demolished in 1856

The Town Hall

The earliest reference to 'le Tolhows', also known as the Common Hall, occurs in 1451,[1] although we have no way of knowing how long the building had stood on the site. In the confusion over the early charters, the name 'Shippewaya' or 'Sypweia' was borrowed from Hythe, and applied to the building in the 1566 and 1579 Constitutions and the 1575 charter.

The Common Hall was the centre of borough administration, where the Bailiffs and Burgesses, dressed in '. . . gownes half in gold and fasshion as in other lyke Corporacons'[2] were sworn into office, with all the other officials on 29th September each year. Here the Bailiffs held '. . . all manner of courts, pleas, causes and matters whatsoever'. These included Great Courts once a quarter, and general courts to maintain law and order and the Borough Constitutions, and to admit new Freemen who were qualified by apprenticeship, birth and residence.

The Common Hall was the first floor of the Toll House, and there are frequent references, in the 15th and 16th centuries, to the '. . . shop under the Common Hall' and 'the Toll House shop'.[3] From the early 17th century the Common Hall, Gaol, House of Correction and Workhouse, formed a complex of buildings on the site of the present Town Hall. An adjoining house was purchased in 1608, and converted into a Gaol and House of Correction.[4] By 1634, a new building had been erected, probably on the north side of the Toll House, the first floor of which was to be used '. . . for the benefit of the Freemen' and the ground floor as a '. . . prison and gayle for the saffe and sure keepinge of prisoners'.[5] Also on the same site was the '. . . ancient workhouse adjoining to the Gaol', recorded in the 1649 meeting of the Corporation.[6] The workhouse was not mentioned in the 1608 or 1634 abuttals of the Gaol, and so must have been either the earlier House of Correction, or part of the ground floor Toll House.

The whole building was rebuilt in the Georgian style in 1757. The Rev. John Price, Keeper of the Bodleian Library, visited Eye in that year and recorded in his diary 'A Town Hall just built, the inside not yet finish'd'.[7] In 1840 the lower floor was converted into a Corn Exchange, with the Court/Council room and reading room on the first floor.[8]

In 1856 the Corporation decided that the Corn Hall was '. . . altogether unsuitable . . . and ill adapted to the requirements of the Town'.[9] The original plan was to build a new Corn Hall to the south of the Town Hall. The Corporation, however, eventually decided to demolish the Town Hall and rebuild on the same site. In July 1856 the site was cleared, and until April 1857 the Corporation met in the Assembly Room.[10] The clock in the old Town Hall was dismantled and later placed in the new clock tower.[11] The Georgian door from the old Town Hall is now the front door of Dove House restaurant in Lambseth Street.

The new Town Hall was designed by Edward Buckton Lamb of Manchester Square, London. Lamb is now regarded as one of the 'Rogue Architects' of the mid Victorian period, and 'His originality and imaginative unorthodoxy as well as his preference and handling of contrasting untreated material textures have made him notorious'.[12] For the Town Hall, Lamb used alternate bands of red and white brick and lozenges of small uncut flints, and topped the clock tower with an ogee roof, with a cupola and vane. Nickolaus Pevsner's opinion of the building was '. . . the horrible Town Hall of 1857, with a horrible tower'.[13]

The foundation stone was laid 18th August 1856, and the building officially opened 12th May 1857.[14] Sir Edward Clarence Kerrison M.P. contributed £1,000 in money and materials, towards the total cost of £2,500. In appreciation of his contribution Sir Edward was presented with a large portrait of himself, painted by Robert Mendham of Eye. On the ground floor of the building were the large corn hall, with bas-relief portraits of Sir Edward and Lady Caroline Kerrison, erected in 1887[15] and a reading room and library. The latter two rooms subsequently became a Court Room and Ante-Room, and are now the cloakrooms and kitchen. On the first floor was the Council Chamber, which was also sometimes used as a Magistrates Court.

A new clock and bell turret were given by Charles Tacon, to commemorate Queen Victoria's Diamond Jubilee, and started by him in November 1897.[16] The small bell in the turret dates from c.1350, was made in London, and was probably the pre–reformation Sanctus Bell from the Church.[17]

Today the former corn hall is used for a wide range of social and charitable functions, and the Council Chamber is still used for its original purpose.

The Gaol

A prison, or gaol had formed part of the castle buildings since at least the early 13th century, until the 16th century. The 1575 Charter granted the Bailiffs the right to have '. . . one prison or gaol, for the safety and safe keeping of all and singular persons that are to be taken or arrested in the said town', although this was obviously a confirmation of earlier grants.

In 1608 the Bailiffs and Burgesses purchased the house of John Cullham, which adjoined the north-east corner of the Toll House, and converted it into the Borough gaol.[1] Part of the building was converted into a House of Correction, possibly after the Poor Law Acts of 1609–10 which ordered them to be built. They were for 'short, sharp, shock' punishment to correct the behaviour of rogues, vagrants, 'lewd women' and parents who deserted their children. In 1634, the ground floor of a new building on the north side of the Toll House became the prison. An inventory of 1634 shows that the prisoners were fettered with a variety of shackles and chains, to large blocks of wood called 'claggs'. The prisoners were set to work 'bunching' or beating and combing flax and hemp. The raw materials, equipment and the market bushel, were all kept in a stockhouse within the building.[2]

In 1817 the building was '. . . very much out of repair and unfit for the safe custody of prisoners'.[3] A new Gaol was built on the north side of the workhouse on Castle Hill. The Gaol consisted of a dayroom, two cells and an adjoining airing yard on the ground floor, and two day rooms for females on the first floor. The entrance was from inside the workhouse, and the office of Gaoler was therefore also held by the Master of the workhouse.[4]

The Gaol was used for short sentences of under three months, passed by the Eye Magistrates. Prisoners awaiting trial at the next Quarter Sessions or Assizes were sent to Ipswich Gaol. As there was only accommodation for a maximum of 4 prisoners, they were not set to work, but had the use of the airing yard for up to 8 hours a day. All the prisoners were allowed Bibles, Prayer Books and other religious works to read: the diet was of 1 1/2lb bread, and at least 3oz. of cheese each day; the female prisoners slept in the workhouse and exercised in the Gaol day rooms.[5] The average number of commitments was only 13 a year in the period 1830–35.

Following the Municipal Corporations Act of 1835, the borough had to contribute towards the financial support of the County Gaol at Ipswich. The Corporation therefore decided, in July 1837, to close the Gaol and let the building to the Hartismere Guardians as an addition to the workhouse.[6]

Workhouses

The earliest rate levied to support the poor of Eye, seems to have been in 1593, when a purse was also purchased to hold the money.[1] Several buildings, owned by the borough and charity trustees, were used to accommodate the poor from the late 16th century, including the former Magdalen Hospital, a workhouse and various town houses.

By 1649 the 'ancient' workhouse adjoining the Gaol, had fallen into disuse. As we saw earlier the workhouse may have been the House of Correction, or part of the ground floor of the Toll House, which was the oldest building on the site. In 1649 the Bailiffs decided that the building should once more become the workhouse and that the Town Gaoler, should also be the Governor of the workhouse at £4 a year. They also ordered £10 to be spent on a stock of '. . . materialls to be used to sett such pore on work'.[2] The borough paid for hemp to be cultivated on Magdalen Hempland, and the poor at the workhouse 'bunched', or beat, and reeled the resulting fibre.

The workhouse was later situated in a building at the west end of the inner bailey of the castle, although the exact date is unknown. However, by 1794 the workhouse, which had an average of 25–30 resident paupers,[3] was '. . . very ruinous and decayed' and a '. . . large and substantial workhouse' was erected on the same site.[4] In 1803 there were 25 paupers, who earnt £115 towards the £564 that it cost to maintain them.[5]

The borough was Incorporated in 1794, under the terms of Gilberts Act of 1781–2. This remained the basis for the management of the poor until 1828 when the Incorporation was dissolved, and the poor came under the care of the parish Churchwardens and Overseers.[6] A new Borough Gaol was built on the north side of the workhouse in 1817, and the Governor, following the Eye tradition, was also the Gaoler.

Under the new Poor Law of 1834, Eye became one of the two workhouses for the 32 parishes of Hartismere Union formed in 1835. Adult and infant paupers were maintained at Eye, and children at the training school at Wortham, where they were taught to make clothing and shoes.

The workhouse was run by a Board of Guardians, representing each parish in the Union, and financed by a Poor Rate levied throughout the Union. Under the regulations of the Poor Law Commissioners in London, the poor could only obtain relief by entering the workhouse, and were there separated into able-bodied or infirm men and women. The workhouse was staffed by a governor, matron, nurse, porter and cook, with a part-time chaplain and surgeon.

The New Poor Law provoked much argument and debate, especially about the treatment of the poor and society's moral responsibility towards them. Those against the Poor Law sought to publicise any allegation of ill treatment, in order to have the law amended. One such allegation made by the Rector of Stoke Ash, and published in *The Times* in 1838, related to Eye.[7] As a result the Poor Law Commissioners investigated complaints about the diet, clothing, medical care, condition of the wards and punishment, but found all was in order.

The Hartismere Guardians and Eye Town Council were divided in their views about the effect of the Law. In February 1837 Sir Augustus Henniker, Chairman of the Guardians, published the following resolution '. . . That since the formation of the Union and by the gradual and temperate enforcement of the regulations of the Poor Law Commissioners the condition and moral character of the labouring classes have been improved; indolence and profligacy has been checked; industry encouraged; more regular and more constant employment obtained. The aggregate assessment of rates for the 32 parishes . . . shows a saving of more than 40% . . . That this reduction has been made chiefly among the class of able-bodied paupers, who are earning their livelihood by the wages of industrious labour, instead of subsisting upon the degrading and demoralising wages of paupers.'[8]

In March 1837 the Mayor and Corporation published their resolution, '. . . readily acknowledging that beneficial effects have resulted from the Act . . . both in checking abuses . . . and giving a facility to the migration of families . . . Yet . . . great as such advantages may have been, they are not commensurate with the evil and cruelty that, by other operations of this Act, debase the character of the honest upright and industrious poor . . . who may by a temporary want of employ . . . be taken from his home and confined within the walls of a Union House.'[9]

The 1794 workhouse was '. . . considerably altered and enlarged'[10] as a Union Workhouse between 1835 and 1839. The architect was William Mason of London,[11] who also designed the

Hartismere Union House, Castle Hill c.1880. Eastern facade of 1854, with the earlier buildings of 1794 and 1835–9 at the rear.

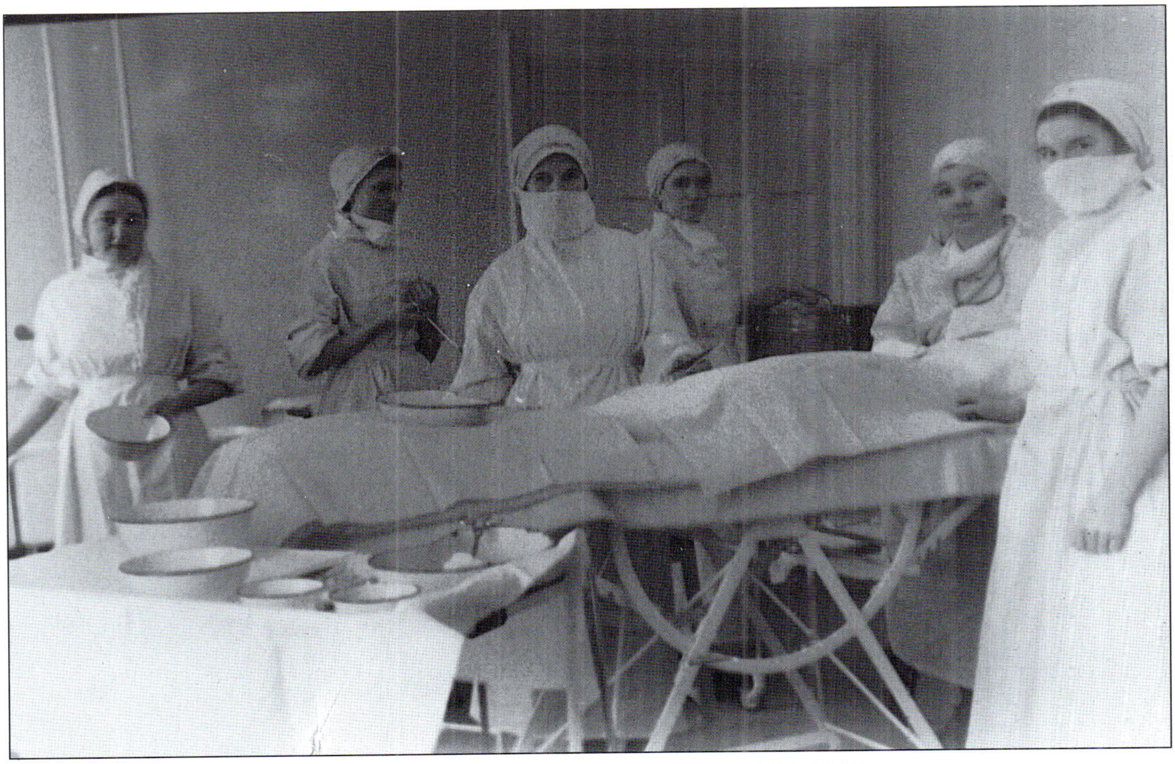

Hartismere Hospital, operating theatre, Second World War.

workhouse at Ipswich in 1836–37, and Tendring in Essex in 1838. The 1839 Tithe Map shows the Union Workhouse built around a square, with openings on the east and north sides. It is impossible from the block plan, to distinguish the 1794 building and the additions of the 1830s. The census returns show there were 56 paupers in 1841 and 168 in 1851.

In 1854 the workhouse was '. . . considerably enlarged by the erection of a new building, at a cost of £4,000, with room for 200 adult paupers'.[12] The new work comprised several wings including a laundry and chapel, and an elaborate main entrance facade to the east. Because of the three stages of development, the workhouse had a complex plan of wings and courtyards, which did not conform to the usual Poor Law Commissioner's designs.

The accommodation was now sufficient for 350 paupers, although the numbers seem rarely to have exceeded 180. The census returns show there were 125 paupers in 1861, 102 in 1871, 179 in 1881, 99 in 1891, 100 in 1901 and 130 in 1911. Between 1896 and 1900, a cottage home, for up to 30 pauper children of school age, was established at Willow House in Castle Street. There were 15 children in the home in 1901, 17 in 1911, 16 in 1921 and 21 in 1931.

The workhouse buildings were in such bad condition before the First World War, that the Local Government Board in July 1912, threatened the Guardians with the dissolution of the Union, unless they erected a new workhouse.[13] The Liberal Government of 1905–14 had introduced reform to social policy, including Old Age Pensions in 1908, and National Insurance in 1911. The result was that fewer people needed workhouse relief, except for the elderly, sick and mentally ill. A census taken in January 1913 shows that of the 123 inmates, 41% were sick, 29% elderly and infirm, 13% mentally ill, 8% infants under 3 years, 4% women in the lying-in ward, and only 5% were able bodied paupers.[14]

In November 1912, the Guardians purchased land adjacent to the road to Mellis as the site of the new Institution, and building work started in September 1913. The Poor Law Institution, also known as the Infirmary, and now as Hartismere Hospital, was to have accommodation for 140 inmates. The design of the building was based on a similar infirmary built in 1912, at Attleborough for Weyland Union. The paupers moved into the new Infirmary in October and November 1916.[15]

The old site and buildings were conveyed to the Town Council in 1917. The 1794 building and most of the 1830s and 1854 additions were subsequently demolished, and part of the remaining buildings converted into temporary council houses by March 1920.[16] In 1924 the old east facade was converted into six council houses[17] and between 1922 and 1928 a further six council houses were built to the west. In 1979 the entire site was cleared and the new curving range of 20 houses erected in 1980.

In the Infirmary the inmates were divided, women on one side of the ground floor, men on the other. The wards were above, staffed by a few nurses who worked extremely long hours, with only two nights off in two months' night duty. One former nurse remembers the striped dresses of the women inmates, the way the inmates filed in for breakfast in silence and the meagre food served on long scrubbed trestle tables. The patients had no cooked meals on Sundays, and the nurses had to fetch hot water from the kitchen to wash the patients. Inmates were taken out for walks on Saturday afternoons.

The washing-up and other menial tasks were carried out by inmates, who also worked in the laundry or in the extensive grounds where vegetables and fruit were grown and pigs kept. The vagrants who slept at the Poor Law Institution would be expected to do a few hours work each morning. Some would follow the horses around the town collecting manure for the vegetable garden! There were 111 residents in 1921 and 119 in 1931.

In 1930 the Poor Law came to an end, and the responsibilities of the Hartismere Guardians were taken over the by East Suffolk County Council. During the Second World War the building was used as a military hospital and for a long period afterwards, minor operations were carried out there. One ward of the Infirmary was a TB Ward until the early 1950s.

The introduction of the National Health Service in 1948 led to the appointment of a geriatrician to the hospital and from then on, instead of patients 'going in to die', rehabilitation became important. The geriatric hospital now has rehabilitation, physiotherapy and occupational therapy units. The spacious maternity block was built in 1970.

Magdalen Hospital

The earliest reference to the leper hospital of St Mary Magdalen occurs in 1329. In that year, and again in 1337, licence was granted to '. . . Adam Frаunceis master, and the brethren of the hospital of St Mary Magdalen for lepers, without the town of Eye and their messengers collecting alms about the realm, they having nothing of their own whereon to live.[1]

The site of the hospital is uncertain. The 1883 Ordnance Survey map has it located to the north of Magdalen Street in the old station goods yard. On the 1839 Tithe Map, however, two fields now part of the Cemetery, are called Magdalen Field. This location would fit with both the early 14th century description given above and that of Jacques Blondell in 1492 who gave '. . . 3d to every sick person in the lazer house at the townshend' [2]

In 1458 the Chamberlains, who were responsible for the letting and supervision of the town moor, built a new bridge called 'le spetel brydge'.[3] This again indicates the hospital was situated at the edge of the town adjacent to the town moor. Between 1387 and 1529 local people made bequests of money, food and building materials to the 'lepers' and 'poor people' in the 'spital', 'lazer house' or 'house of the Blessed Mary Magdalen of Eye'.

After the Dissolution, the hospital passed into the control of the town Bailiffs. A lease between the Bailiffs and Paul Stevenson of Eye in 1604, stipulates that the latter shall have the lease of '. . . their hospitall called St Mary Magdalen'. The land belonging to the hospital was to provide an income towards the keeping of '. . . all such poore sick aged lame and diseased . . with leprosye or any other foule contagious diseases, sicknesses or imbecilities, and all such as shallbe decrepite, aged and decayed persons'.[4]

The building, later known as 'Magdalen Almshouse', was used as a poor house until the mid-18th century. A list of charity properties drawn up 1758–90 records that the Hospital was '. . . so very ruinous that the trustees lately took it down'.[5]

Magdalen Street c.1880. Police Station on right; the thatched cottages on the left were demolished in 1921 and replaced by the council houses.

Bedingfield Almshouses

In the 1620s Nicholas Bedingfield of Swattis Hall, Gislingham, purchased from John Austin a complex of buildings and land '. . . abutting west on Lamsey Street and north on the river at Lamsey Ford . . .'.[1] He converted them into almshouses, known as 'Poor Austins' or 'Bedingfield's Almshouses', for four poor widows or old maids of Eye. Sometime before 1636 Nicholas had demolished the building as it was 'ruinous' and a new brick house was built on the site. In his will of 1636 he described the building as a '. . . brickhouse new built for the habitation of poor women'.[2]

The endowment to support the charity comprised land at Cranley, two cottages and a house, later to become the Bedingfield Arms, next to the Almshouses. Each woman was to receive 2s a month, two cart loads of wood a year, and a grey gown every two or three years. Any surplus income was to be used to maintain the building, and to give extra relief to the poor women who were '. . . most feeble and disabled by great age and sickness'.[3]

At the time of the Charity Commissioners' report in 1830, there were 8 women in the Almshouse, which was in a very bad state of repair, and being used as a parish poor house for paupers, rather than a selective almshouse. The Almshouses were returned to their original use after the New Poor Law Act of 1834, when outdoor relief was prohibited, and all paupers had to go into the Union workhouse.

The Almshouses were rebuilt in 1850, and were restored and converted into dwellings for 3 widows in the 1970s. The 'gothic' front has scrolls with the inscription 'Rebuilt, Anno Domini MDCCCL'. The original Almshouse had the following phrases and words, which have been placed over the doors and windows, 'Believe Right; Doe Well; Avoid Ill for Heaven, Amen; Povertie; Humilitie; Patience and Charitie'.

Bedingfield Almshouses, founded 1636, rebuilt 1850.

Lithographed by Albert Betts, Mortlake.

Printed by W. W. Sprague & Co. London. E.C.

EYE GRAMMAR SCHOOL, EYE, SUFFOLK.

JAMES K. COLLING, ARCHT.

The Grammar School and Guildhall

The origins of the Grammar School date from c.1495, although there are references to a school in the 1450s.[1] In 1488 John Fisk bequeathed £53 6s 8d to the Guilds of St Mary and St Peter in Eye, to purchase land to maintain a Guild or Chantry Priest in Eye.[2] The land had to be purchased within four years of his death, which occurred in 1491, or the bequest would be void.

Sometime between 1530 and 1532 Thomas Golding, vicar of Eye 1489–1529, then vicar of Barrowby in Lincolnshire, recalled the events surrounding the purchase of the land, in a letter to the Prior, which is worth quoting at length. '. . . we coulde not finde none in no place that was mete for us. I thank Almighty God for it that it was my fortune that I desired John Fanner to breake his fast withe me in the vicaridge the daye before New Year in Christmas, and as we satte by the fyer we comonyd [commented] howe that the towne should lose this service the whiche should be greate rebuke on to all the towne. Then the holy goste putte him in minde . . . "I will selle you (15 acres at Cranley) . . . for 9 score marks" (180 marks or £120) . . . I went into the pulpet the next daye and shewed unto all the parishe that we were like to lose the service . . . "How saye", now said I unto them, "if I have bought a ground for you so that ye may stond in the church yard and see it," and I showed them how I had made a bargaine with John Fanner, and showed them the daies of payment . . . "and if it be a bargaine, because it for the common wele, speake all Una Voce [one voice] and seye ye this was a godly hearing"; every man, woman and child said yea, yea . . .'[3] Money was raised from donations and bequests to the 'priest's service', and the land purchased by the feoffees or trustees in 1495.

The feoffees of the land immediately widened John Fisk's original intention, in order that the chantry priest should also be the master of the town school. In 1495 Thomas Golding went to John Cornwallis of Ling Hall in Brome, and obtained '. . . a grant or licence that no Grammar school should be kept within seven miles, and that they might teach all the seven sciences'.[4] These were grammar, logic, rhetoric, arithmetic, music, geometry and astronomy.

The establishment of the chantry priest, and the grant of the licence in 1495, marks the foundation of Eye Grammar School, which was to continue for 470 years until 1965. Because the chantry priest was also the schoolmaster, the school was held in the Guildhall next to the church. A yard, adjoining the churchyard, was given by John Upson, for the good of his soul, c.1488.[5] The yard may have formed part of the Guildhall property as the names 'Guildhall' and 'Upson's tenement' are often used for the building.

In the same letter of 1530–32 quoted above, Thomas Golding protested that the feoffment was under threat of being lost '. . . my mischevos men (who) will break John Fisk's will, and all sowles to be unprayed for', and appealed to the Prior in order that '. . . the sowles shall not be deceyved'. As a result of this protest to the Prior, a new feoffment was drawn up in 1533.

Thomas Blow, one of the Bailiffs, in 1535 '. . . did cut in sunder' the 1495 licence, and '. . . made measure of it for a tailor'.[6] However, the Chantry Certificate of 1548 shows that the '. . . scoole hath contynued tyll Michaelmas 1547', but was now without a master, as one could not be found.[7]

As Chantries had been abolished in 1547, the next master to be appointed was a layman, Robert Shene, who was also parish clerk. An unknown commentator on the events of the Reformation in Eye, writing in the reign of Queen Mary, noted '. . . whan thes layeman had the service than goddes service began to decay in the chirche, and the scholars were not so dilygently applyed and taughte, neyther in nurture or in lernyng of vertu and good maners'.[8]

In the Autumn of 1556 the Bishop of Norwich ordered Sir William Cordell of Long Melford, and Sir Edward Waldegrave of Bures to investigate the Bailiffs of Eye for '. . . abusyng of ther Town Land'. After examining the relevant deeds and papers, Sir William decided that the '. . . chief intent and purpose' had been for a chantry priest, but also that there was another meaning in the intention of the donors, '. . . that the same preste suld be a Scolemaster and lernyd in latyn tunng, to teache and trayne up the yowught of the towne in good lernyng and vertu'.[9] The Bailiffs agreed to return to having a priest as the Schoolmaster in the future. In 1566, however, they changed the qualification to that of '. . . a learned man apt to teach a Grammar School'. Over the next 400 years, clergymen occupied the position of schoolmaster for less than 80 years.

The 1566 Borough Constitutions included regulations for the school.[10] The pupils were to

'. . . learn the grammar and latin tongue' and had to be able to read Latin and English before they were admitted. The schoolmaster was to receive £10 a year, and had also to maintain the church choir when required, and present a comedy or tragedy performed by the scholars once a year. He also had to ensure that the scholars attended church on Sundays and holy days. In 1650 the master and scholars were described as '. . . having antiently satt on the north side of the chauncell'.[11]

A bequest by Francis Kent of Oxbcrough in Norfolk, in 1593, extended the educational provision to 'elementary' as well as 'secondary' levels.[12] Kent's bequest comprised a house and 26 acres of land in Bedfield and Worlingworth, the income from which was to maintain an Usher, or second master, at Eye Grammar School. He was to teach grammar and writing to the children of Eye, Horham, Athelington and Bedfield, who were to '. . . learn Grammar until such time as they shall have learned to say by harte all the English Rules in the Queene's Grammar, and can reasonably construe the Latin Rules, and also to wright'.

The first Usher, William Lambert, was appointed in 1599.[13] The Bailiffs and Burgesses drew up rules for the Usher in 1600.[14] He was to behave himself as '. . . underteacher and inferior to the mayster'; to be under the direction of the master as to the method of teaching, and the school hours; and to be able to write Secretary and Roman hands; and to teach writing and casting of accounts.

In 1614 Edward Mallows bequeathed £200 to help maintain two or three scholars from Eye at Cambridge University.[15]

In the mid-17th century the salary of the Master was £16 and that of the Usher £12 a year. The school was described as 'very low' in 1672, when the position of master and Usher were united '. . . until the school shall increase',[16] which it did in 1675. Thomas Brown, who had been Master since before 1650 until 1672, subsequently opened a private school in the district. In 1675 he was invited to return as Master and to 'bring his boarders with him, which it is hoped may bee a good means to restore the schoole, which is nowe decayed and near to nothing'.[17]

Under Brown, the school seems to have been kept as a private, rather than a public school, although Brown received the salary for being Master and Usher. In 1681 James Harvey of Eye, one of the feoffees of the school charities, protested to the other feoffees that '. . . for some yeares past there hath bin no publique school kept for the said towne nor either Scholemaster or Usher . . . for the publique benefitt of the said towne according to the originall foundation of the said Schole and the intent of the guifts for manitenace there . . .'.[18]

The outcome of the protest is unknown, but it seems Brown or his pupils left, as in 1692 the school was '. . . not so great but that one man might well discharge both the places of Master and Usher'. The salary was then £36 a year, being £20 as Master and £16 as Usher. The united office continued from 1692–1876 with an average salary of £18 a year. The School had an 'English Schoolmaster' 1738–88,[19] indicating that only English was being taught, which was contrary both to the foundation and the Borough Constitutions.

In 1822 the school seems to have been put on a new footing when Rev. John Knevett was appointed Master at £20 a year.[20] He was to teach 20 boys to read, to write, the common rules of arithmetic, to Catechise and accompany the boys to church on Fridays and Sundays. The 20 boys were to be educated free, except for books, pens, ink and fuel. He was allowed to take a further 20 fee-paying boys and 4 boarders for his own profit. The Charity Commissioners Report of 1830 shows that Knevett had 20 free scholars and 18–20 fee-paying day boys, who were taught the 3 Rs, Geography and Land Surveying. There were also 7 boarders who with a few of the day scholars, were also taught Latin in a separate class.[21]

By the Municipal Corporations Act of 1835, the management of the town charities was removed from the Corporation, and placed in the hands of municipal charity trustees. However, the foundation charity had become part of the Corporation income since 1692. The Corporation paid for repairs and maintenance to the Guildhall, and the schoolmaster was paid for from Kent's charity. The Corporation refused to make any contribution towards the school from 1840 until 1876, and the income was therefore limited to Kent's charity, which amounted to £37 a year.

A report was made for the Schools Inquiry Commission in 1867. There were then 23 free and 7 fee-paying scholars at £3 a year who were all the sons of tradesmen and farmers. There were no boarders, but there had been 15 in the 1840s.[22] Part of the Guildhall was the master's residence, and the schoolroom with its '. . . low ceiling and insufficient means of ventilation,

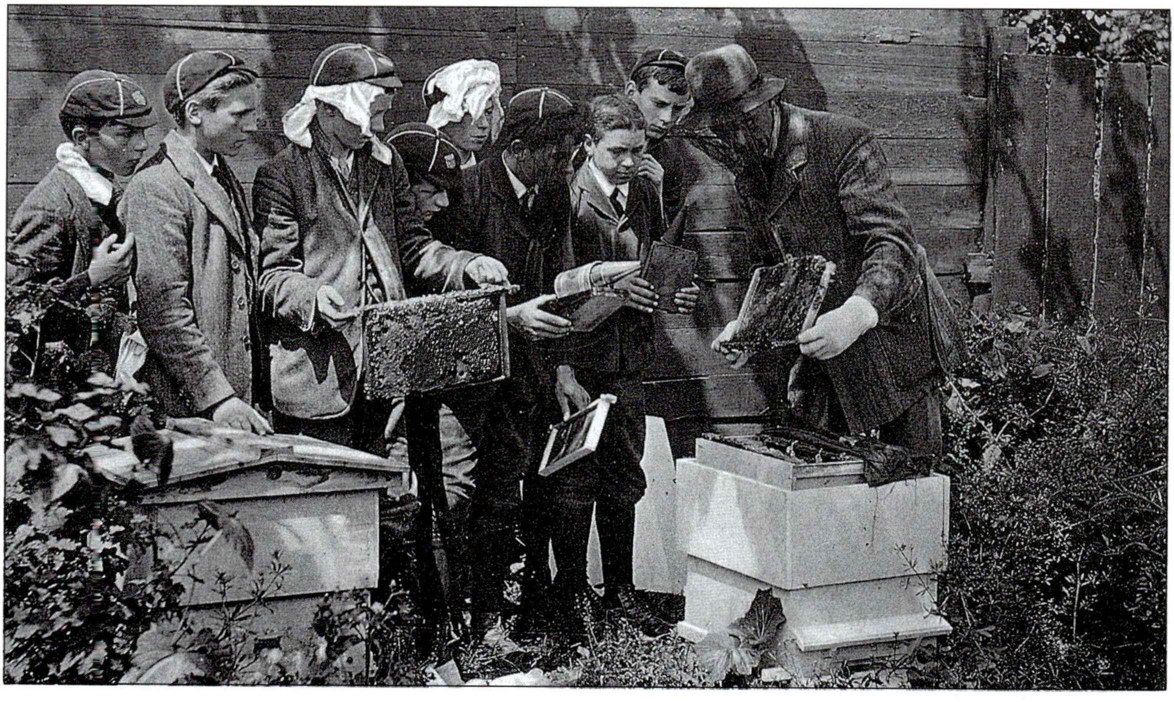

Domestic Economy Room and Bee-Keeping lesson from *School Prospectus,* 1916.

was quite filled by the 30 boys present'. The boys were divided into two classes, and were tested by the Commission's Inspector. He found that pupils in the senior class could only work simple rules of arithmetic; their spelling was only average for a village school; there was little progress in history or geography; not one pupil could parse a simple sentence; and none had learnt Latin. The lower class was '. . . exceedingly backward and ignorant', and apart from simple arithmetic and erratic spelling '. . . it cannot be said that they know anything'.

The Inspector, Mr Richmond, noted that there was no discontent in Eye about the state of the school, which was now no more than an elementary school. He found it was never visited nor examined except by the master, and that the parents seemed to care little about their sons' education. '. . . If it is to be redeemed to real usefulness, the first impulse must come from without, for the attitude of the borough is one of perfect quiescence'.

The Endowed Schools Act of 1868 provided the impulse with the prospect of a new scheme for the administrations of the school's endowments. The resignation of Rev. Charles Notley, master from 1837 in 1874, and the appointment of Sir Edward Clarence Kerrison as Chairman of the trustees gave a further impetus to the school.

Lady Caroline Kerrison paid for the restoration of the Guildhall by the architect James Colling in 1875. The building was stripped down to the frame and the interior redesigned. The Guildhall became the residence of the Master and 15–20 boarders, and a new schoolroom was built on the adjoining site. The Kerrisons paid £1,170 of the total cost of £1,450, and their coat of arms was carved on the sill of the middle oriel window on the south side, and those of Eye on the west gable window of the Guildhall.[23]

In 1876, a new scheme for the school's endowments combined the foundation charity, Kent's and Mallow's gifts into a single trust.[24] The school now became fee paying, and boys were admitted at 8 years after an examination, and left at 15 years of age. Boys from Eye, Horham, Athelington and Bedfield were to have precedence over all other applicants. The curriculum was brought up to date and included the 3 Rs, Geography, History, Land Surveying, Latin, a European Language, Natural Science, Drawing and Vocal Music.

Further additions to the school accommodation included a new wing to the school house in 1876, a dining hall in 1882, and the acquisition of the adjoining house by 1885 when there were 40 day and 30 boarding pupils.

A new scheme for the school was agreed in 1909 when the East Suffolk County Council took control of the school, as a County Secondary School for girls as well as boys.[25] The age range was now from 8 to 18 years, and 25% of the senior pupils were to have free scholarships awarded, by the County Council, to pupils sitting an examination aged 11–13 years. In 1910, there were 20 boarders and 44 day pupils, with a staff of a Headmaster, three Assistants and one part-time Assistant.

In 1911 most of the school buildings, except the Guildhall, were demolished, and new premises built, with accommodation for 100 pupils, at the cost of £4,000. The buildings were designed by Joseph Webb, Education Surveyor to East Suffolk County Council, and were opened in December 1911.[26] The building, which was altered and extended after 1974, still has the Arms of Eye, flanked by the Tudor emblems of a Garter and Rose on the front. The facilities included 5 classrooms, dining hall, dormitories, library, bathrooms, sanitorium and a chemistry laboratory. Manual instruction was given in woodwork and gardening for boys, and cookery and laundry for girls. The first girls entered the school in 1912 and by 1914 there were 8 girl and 17 boy boarders, 43 girl and 35 boy day pupils, and a staff comprising the Headmaster and seven Assistants.

Between 1916 and 1925 the land belonging to Kent's and Mallow's charities was sold, and the funds used to purchase new playing fields.

The school prospectus of c.1930 lists the subjects as English, French, Mathematics, Surveying, Physics, Chemistry, Botany, Nature Study, History, Geography, Vocal Music, Dancing and Physical Training which included Old English Folk Dancing. In addition there were Agricultural Science, Experimental Gardening, Beekeeping and Woodwork for boys; and Hygiene, First Aid and Housewifery for girls.[27]

The school ceased to be fee paying after the 1944 Education Act, the pupils now having to pass the 11+ examination. In 1965, against much local opposition, the school was closed and the pupils were transferred to Diss and Stowmarket. The last Headmaster was Mr Eric Crinean who had been in office since 1937.

The buildings subsequently became St Peter and St Paul, Church of England Aided Primary

School. In May 1966 the two senior classes moved from Castle Hill,[28] and for several years the school operated from the two sites. In 1974 and again in 1979 the buildings were extended, and the Castle Hill premises, which had been the National School since 1839, were closed in July 1979. The extensions to the Primary School were dedicated by the Bishop of Dunwich in 1979.

Eye National School. The left range of the large building was erected by Sir Edward Kerrison in 1839, and extended in 1859 and 1872. The Infants' Room to the right was built in 1872. The buildings ceased to be used in 1979, and were demolished in 1987.

Eye National School, with Frederick Bray Headmaster for 33 years, 1888–1921.

Occupations and Industries

The earliest mention of trade in Eye was in 1673, when Richard Blome recorded that 'Eye is a pretty large market town . . . its market, which is but small, the trade being now drawn to Diss, is on Saturday. The women's employ in this town is making of bone lace.'[1] This latter phrase was repeated in all the subsequent guide books and directories until 1829.

Pigot's Directory of 1830 notes that '. . . the town's business is of a domestic nature, and some of the humbler class of industrious females employ themselves in lace making. Here are a few well furnished shops and an extensive brewery'. The 1865 Directory records that, '. . . a good trade was carried out in this town some years ago in the making of pillow lace, which gave employment to the women and children of agricultural labourers, but since the introduction of machines it has become nearly extinct'.[2]

Several Flemish-style lace bobbins, with single necks and bulbous ends, have been found at Apple Tree Cottage, the former Pest House; Dove House; Maynards the Chemists; and 24 Church Street where an 18th-century parchment lace pattern was also found. All the bobbins were discovered behind chimneys or in ceiling voids, places usually associated with superstitiously protecting houses from evil.

It seems that Eye, and perhaps Yaxley, were the centre of a localised lace industry, which died out earlier than in other areas of the country, because the simple designs could easily be made by machinery.[3] The last lace maker in Eye died about 1914.[4]

In the 19th century there was in Eye the usual range of agricultural occupations, trades, shops and professions common in all rural market towns. The major employers were the Lambseth Street and Wellington Road maltings and breweries which are detailed in the next section, and the Flax Rettery works.

The flax works employed a large number of people between 1851 and 1872. Sir Edward Kerrison was the driving force behind the establishment of the Hartismere Flax Association in 1851. He encouraged the growing of flax by his tenant farmers, with the result that over 5,000 acres were under cultivation by 1864. Sir Edward built the Rettery in 1851, which was situated between the present Fire Station and the river. The works were leased to Messrs Chase Brothers, who employed about 80 people in 1855, and between 250 and 300 in 1864, working at the 45 scutching (pounding) mills and in the carding room. The works were destroyed by fire in May 1864, rebuilt in Hoxne Road by Sir Edward, and opened in December of the same year.[5] The works closed about 1872 because '. . . in consequence of the low price of wool and cotton Mr Chase found he could not carry on the work at a profit'.[6]

Garood and Sons, iron and brass founders and agricultural implement makers were situated behind No. 18 Lowgate Street, c.1844–1908. The long tiled shed of the foundry and the chimney still survive. Collins, machinists, iron and brass founders in Wellington Road from c.1883, were succeeded by Elijah Young and Co. c.1900–4, who in turn were succeeded by Bob Ford in the 1940s. George Day, wheelwrights, blacksmiths, church bell frame makers and hangers were situated in Wellington Road. The firm was established in 1802, and seem to have started bell hanging in the 1860s, and continued until just after the Second World War. Throughout this period, the firm was responsible for restoring frames and hanging bells in numerous churches in Norfolk and Suffolk.

The Eye Gas Light and Coke Company was established in 1850, with the intention of providing 120 private lights and 30 street lights. Mr Samuel Chapell of Harlestone, Ironmonger and Engineer erected '. . . a Gasometer and all other necessary operations and buildings for lighting the Town of Eye with gas'.[7] The red brick Gas Works, on the south side of Magdalen Street, were built in 1850 and the gas pipes laid and the street lights erected in the same year. The base of the former street light in Broad Street, near the site of the Kerrison Memorial, had the inscription 'AD 1850 – Presented by Eye Gas Co', and gave the distances from Eye to eight local towns. One of the employees was also the town lamp lighter, who each evening had to light all the street lights with an oil torch on the end of a long pole.

The Gas Works were enlarged in 1872 and the private company continued until 1922 when, to prevent the closure of the works, the enterprise was purchased by the Borough Council.[8] A detailed survey of the works in August 1939 revealed that '. . . owing to the condition of the Gas Works it would be dangerous to continue to make gas . . until the retorts had been renewed and the new main laid'.[9] In the same month, the Council applied to the Board of

Trade to be allowed to close the Gas Works, on the grounds that it was unprofitable and that electricity had been available in the Borough since 1933. In 1991 British Gas brought a natural gas supply to Eye from the Diss Gas Compressor Station, situated on Eye Airfield!

The following analysis shows the businesses in Eye mentioned in the 1844 and 1937 Directories, and records only the main trade of each business. Following the trade the first figure represents 1844 and the second 1937.

Auctioneers 1, 1; Bakers 5, 2; Banks 3, 2; Booksellers and printers 2, 2; Blacksmiths 4, 1; Boot and shoe makers 6, 5; Brewers 2, 1; Builders 4, 5; Butchers 4, 2; Carriers 4, 2; Cattle dealers 1, 1; Chemists 2, 2; Corn chandlers 1, 3; Drapers 4, 4; Farmers 28, 21; Grocers, 5, 5; Hairdressers 3, 1 Gents and 2 Ladies; Insurance agents 6, 2; Ironmongers 3, 1; Millers 3, 1; Painters and plumbers 2, 1; Publicans 13, 11; Schools 7, 3; Shopkeepers 3, 2; Solicitors 3, 3; Surgeons 5, 2; Tailors 6, 1; Watchmakers 3, 1; Wheelwrights 2, 1.

Trades that occurred in 1844 but had disappeared by 1937 were a basket maker, 7 beerhouse keepers, 6 carpenters, a coach maker, a cooper, a dyer, a glass and china dealer, 4 milliners, 3 saddlers, 2 straw hat makers, a stone mason, 2 tinners and braziers, 2 veterinary surgeons, and 2 wine and spirit merchants.

Trades that were present in Eye in 1937, but not in 1844 were an agricultural implement maker, a coal merchant, an egg collecting agency for Sainsburys, 2 dental surgeons (1 and 2 days a week), a firewood dealer, a fishmonger, 2 fish and chip shops, 2 fruiterers, a furniture dealer, 2 garages, a haulage contractor, a horse breeder, a motor cycle dealer, a daily omnibus, a firm of pastry cooks and a wireless dealer.

George Day, bell frame-makers, Wellington Road, c.1925.

Kerrison School Band, outside White Lion Hotel, c.1910.

The 'Queen's Head'; Arthur Palmer, publican, c.1902–c.1914.

Breweries and Public Houses

There were two breweries in Eye from at least the mid-16th century, until the early 20th century. The 1566 Constitutions imposed fines on the victuallers (publicans) who did not purchase beer from the two town brewhouses. The Bailiffs deemed such action as '. . . unneighbourly and to the manifest prejudice of pore people . . . who are sett awork . . . in buting the small wort and small beer . . .'.[1]

The Bailiffs granted licences to victuallers and alehouse keepers, allowing them to 'sell food and beer at reasonable prices'. The licence could be revoked if the recipient allowed unlawful games to be played, or did '. . . harbor lodge or keep any rogues, vagabonde, ydell or suspected persons' or '. . . suffer any evell rule within hys sayde house'.[2]

The 19th and 20th-century County Directories, from 1823 to 1937, give details of the breweries and Public Houses in Eye. All the dates in the following paragraphs are those of the Directories.

The major maltings and brewery were situated off the west side of Lambseth Street, in the area of Tacon Close, and had a railway siding to the nearby station. In 1784 the brewery was owned by John Jacob, who was declared a bankrupt in 1801 at which time there were 25 public houses, in and around Eye, belonging to the brewery.[3] The business was taken over by Robert Cobbold, who was succeeded 1830–39 by Richard and Charles Tacon. The Tacon brothers sold the premises to Harwood and Co. 1879–83, who in turn sold to the Colchester Brewery 1885–8. The brewery continued until 1908–12, when, apart from the stores, the whole business was closed.

The other maltings and brewery were in Wellington Road, although the actual postal address varied from Back Lane, Brewery Road, Wellington Road and Church Street. The building was marked on the 1839 tithe map as the 'new brewery' and was occupied by Flowerdew and Gowing from at least c.1830–9 until c.1844–55. By 1855 the business had been taken over by Benjamin Etheridge who remained until 1873. The premises were then worked by Charles Fisher until 1904 when they were taken by Adnams of Southwold and used as a store. Adnams had their own maltings in Hoxne Road, in the former Rettery works, which was opened 1908–12. Between 1912–16 the Hoxne Road Maltings and part of the Wellington Road premises were sold to Edward Fison Ltd, and the remaining part to Steward and Patterson. This latter building still remains and has been owned by Edward Thompson (Engineering) Ltd since 1949.

The White Lion was the main Inn until its closure in 1986. The name probably derives from the heraldic white lion of the Mortimers and Plantagenets as Earls of March. In 1460 John de la Pole (1442–91), Duke of Suffolk and Lord of the Honour of Eye, married Elizabeth, daughter of Richard Plantagenet, Duke of York, and sister of Edward IV and Richard III. In 1826 David Davy recorded that 'Under the sill of a window . . . is carved an angel holding before him a shield bearing . . . the Arms of de la Pole'.[4]

The White Lion was a Coaching Inn and a Posting Establishment during the 18th and early 19th centuries, with a daily coach service to London, Ipswich and Bungay until c.1840. The Posting Establishment sign still survives around the entrance to the courtyard. Noller's Wagon or Van took passengers and goods, from the White Lion, to London and Norwich three times a week in the 1840s, but the service had ceased by at least 1855.

The Inn was chosen, by the B.B.C. in 1980, as the location for filming *The Diary of an Innkeeper* starring Robert Hardy, in which many local people were involved. The main part of the Inn has been converted into 4 dwellings now called White Lion House, the stables have been converted into 2 'town houses' and other dwellings have been built on the former courtyard and garden.

The 18th-century Adam-style Assembly Room in the courtyard, now the Eye Theatre, made the Inn the centre of fashionable social life in Eye. The earliest mention of the room occurs in January 1739, when a benefit Assembly was held for Mr Samuel Gibbs, the organist of Eye, at '. . . a very handsome new-built Room in Eye'.[5] Here were held all the balls, concerts, banquets, celebration dinners given by newly-elected M.P.s, and commemorations of national events such as Coronations. There was a small musicians' gallery, approached by a ladder at one end of the room.

The number of public and beer houses in Eye has decreased dramatically in the 20th century. In 1844–55 there were 14 public and 5 beer houses; in 1896 a total of 16, in 1937 a total of 11 and in 1993 only the Queen's Head and Red Lion remain. In proportion to the population, the figures represent in 1844–55 one public house per 133 people in Eye; in 1896 one per 129; in 1937 one per 157, and in 1993 one per 870. Some of the pubs to have closed down in recent times include: The Cherry Tree (17 Castle Street, the former dairy); The Star (15 Castle Street, the former café); The Malt and Hops (46 Castle Street); The King's Arms (44 Castle Street); The Railway Tavern and The Crown (Magdalen Street); The Bedingfield Arms (corner of Wellington Road and Lambseth Street); The Cherry Tree (Ludgate Causeway); The Eight Bells (48 Church Street); The Black Swan (now demolished, next to the Queen's Head); The Duke of Wellington (opposite the entrance to Paddock House); The King's Head (3 Church Street); The Bull (3 Lambseth Street); The Bottles (11 The Cross); The Grapes (destroyed by fire, Church Street); The Buck's Horn (7 Buckshorn Lane) and The Horse Shoes (Castle Street).

Eye Station, 1920s.

Communications

Roads

In 1711 the road between Ipswich and Scole, the present A140, became a turnpike or toll road. In the same year a spur from Yaxley to Eye was also turnpiked. In 1802 the present B1079 and B1077 roads between Woodbridge and Eye via Debenham also became a turnpike, terminating at Tollgate House in Lowgate Street.[1]

A daily coach service from Bungay to London, via Eye and Ipswich, called at the White Lion at 9 a.m. and again at 5 p.m. on the return journey. This service ceased between 1839 and 1844, from which time Yaxley on the main road became the halt for Eye. In 1844 Noller's Waggon or Van left the White Lion for London or Norwich on Mondays, Tuesdays and Saturdays; Francis Smith's waggon went to Norwich from the King's Head on Mondays, Thursdays, Fridays and Saturdays; and Robert Dade's went from Magdalen Street to Ipswich on Tuesdays and Saturdays.[2]

Railways

In 1846, the Borough Council opposed the Eastern Union Railway's plan for a railway from Stowmarket to Norwich via Diss, because the line would pass 4 miles from Eye. They predicted that the consequence would be that the '. . . commercial and agricultural interests of upwards of 15,000 persons will be seriously injured and affected'. Instead the Council supported the Norfolk Railway's proposals for a line from Stowmarket to Attleborough or Wymondham via Eye, as it would '. . . materially promote and insure the interests of both commerce and agriculture'.[3]

However, their petition to the House of Commons failed and in 1848–9 the Eastern Union Railway opened their line from Stowmarket to Norwich via Diss, with a station at Mellis to serve Eye. Sir Edward Kerrison, M.P. for Eye and the major landowner, held different views from the Borough Council and opposed any proposals to link Eye with the railway at Mellis, or any other schemes to bring the railway to Eye.

The 1865 Post Office Directory shows there had been a reduction in the carriers' services. William Smith went from Church Street to Ipswich on Tuesdays and Norwich on Wednesdays and Saturdays; and Edward Catchpole, also from Church Street, went daily to Mellis Station.

In 1864, Sir Edward Clarence Kerrison and Lord Henniker supported the proposal to construct a line to link Eye with the main line at Mellis. The market had declined for want of a rail link, and the cost of some goods was kept high by the additional road transport charges from Mellis. For example, the cost of transporting coal was 2s 6d a ton, compared with the estimated 3d a ton by rail.[4] The Mellis and Eye Railway Act was passed in July 1865,[5] and the line opened on 2 April 1867.[6] The line had been financed by the local Mellis and Eye Railway Company, but was staffed and run by the Great Eastern Railway for 50% of the gross receipts.[7]

Hopes were high for the future prosperity of Eye, and comparisons were made with the beneficial effects that the earlier railway had made on the growth of trade in nearby Diss. The construction of the line to Eye had left the local company with a debt of over £6,000, which was not paid off until 1883. The line, however, was profitable from the outset, reaching its peak in 1896.

As traffic increased, a new goods' shed was built in 1885, and a siding to the brewery laid in 1888. David Morley opened his coal, corn, cake seed and manure merchant's business in the station yard c.1874. He was succeeded by Cullum and Sons c.1879, who sold the business to Walter Betts c.1892, and who ceased trading 1929–33. Armine Saville and Co. ran their coal merchant's business from the station yard from c.1879 and were still trading in 1937. Cattle sales were held in the station auction yard, from c.1883, and greatly increased the traffic on the line.

The Mellis and Eye Railway was one of the shortest local branch lines in the country. The line provided a linking shuttle service, with Eye as its terminus, but led nowhere. The failure to get a through line in the 1840s, the 20-year delay in building the branch line, and the failure to link up with the Ipswich to Norwich line at Framlingham all contributed to the increasing isolation of Eye. In 1877 the Great Eastern Railway increased their portion of the receipts to 60%, and finally took over the line in 1898.

The proximity of Diss, on the main line, hindered the growth of Eye and the prosperity of the railway, and indeed still overshadows Eye. As we saw earlier, Richard Blome commented in 1673 that Eye had a small market, because most of the trade was drawn to Diss. The population declined steadily from a peak of 2,587 in 1851, to 2 064 in 1891 and to 1,733 in 1931. Several businesses employing large numbers of workers closed; the flaxworks c.1872; Garoods foundry c.1892; and the Colchester brewery adjoining the station 1908–12. There was no significant increase in traffic or profit on the railway from 1893 to 1920. In 1922 a halt was constructed at Yaxley on the A140, and the staff working the line reduced.

Mr Eldridge, son of the Headmaster of the Grammar School, recalled that in 1926 '. . . There were four passenger trains a day to Mellis, via Yaxley Halt. They consisted of two ancient Great Eastern Railway coaches pulled by a little tank engine. The line to Mellis was single track. The connections to Norwich and Ipswich usually meant a long wait'.[8]

From the outset, there had been a problem in making connections with the fast through trains to Norwich, Ipswich and London, all of which stopped at Diss, but not at Mellis. Passengers either had to travel to Diss for the fast trains, or to Mellis where they could only connect with the slower stopping trains. A daily bus service to Ipswich, and a Friday market service to Diss which started c.1925, took passengers from the railway. General economic depression and competition from the bus services led to the closure of the passenger service on 2nd February 1931.

A daily goods service continued to link Eye to the rail network. Extra trains ran during the sugar beet campaigns, and for the weekly cattle market. During the Second World War the line served Eye airfield, and to a lesser extent Thorpe Abbots and Horham airfields. The sidings at Mellis and Eye were used for storage and unloading.

The line was finally closed for goods traffic on 13th July 1964, as part of the Beeching cuts. Mellis station was closed in 1967, leaving the nearest rail links to Eye at Diss or Stowmarket.

Mail cart, c.1908.

Fairs

In addition to the weekly market there were also annual fairs held in Eye. The Priory held a four-day St Peter's Fair starting on 1 August, the Feast of St Peter's Chains, from the 1080s until 1537.

The Bailiffs of Eye held a three-day fair on Monday, Tuesday and Wednesday of Whit week at Eye; a Lammas Day Fair at Thrandeston on 31 July and 1 August; and a St Bartholomew Fair at Finningham on 24 August.

The Bailiffs as magistrates, had the right '. . . to keep account at the fair for justice, in any bargain or contract made in the same fair by their Court of Piepowder'.[1] This Court derived its name from the Middle English for 'dusty footed', indicating the pedlars and traders attending the fair. In cases of dispute between the itinerant traders and their customers, the Court gave summary, or instant, decisions and justice. For example in 1593, Nicholas Turner of Thornham Magna, tanner, was fined because '. . . he did offer to be sold on Mondaye in Whitsun week, one cheeke of lether, for that it was not sufficiently tanned, according to the statute'.[2]

The Thrandeston and Finningham Fairs were mainly for the sale of sheep and cattle. Both fairs were eventually held at Eye although the names were retained. Thrandeston Fair which had been held at Eye since 1867 was abolished in 1872. Finningham Fair was moved to Eye in 1868 and still held on 24 August. It may have formed the basis of the annual August Horticultural Show, recorded in the 1912 County Directory, which in turn developed into the present Eye Show. The Eye Whit Monday Fair for cattle and toys seems to have ceased between 1900 and 1904.

Garnham's boot and shoe dealers, Broad Street, c.1925. Mr. Charles Ethridge on left.

The Theatre

Various travelling theatre companies performed in Eye in the 18th century, probably in a barn or other suitable building fitted up for the purpose as required. For example in 1784 William Scraggs' Company performed the comedy *The Suspicious Husband* and the farce *The Poor Soldier,* at the New Theatre at Eye.[1] This need not indicate a theatre, but a building used for the four weeks of the season.

David Fisher, who was to dominate an East Anglian theatre circuit, based on the smaller towns joined Scraggs' Company as the manager in 1792.[2] Messrs Fisher and Co's Company of Comedians staged a seven-week season in Eye in 1793 and, in spite of some initial opposition to their application to 'fit up' a theatre, scored a great success. A testimonial published in the Ipswich Journal signed by Thomas Wythe of Park House, and 24 other residents, declared that '. . . the scenes, dresses and decorations are superior to most provincial theatres, and the best testimony of their abilities and good conduct is the continual crowded houses they have experienced . . .'[3] They came again in 1795, their offerings included: 'By desire of Lord Brome, the much admired comedy of *The Dramatist* with the musical farce of *The Prize*, and, by desire of the Worshipful Bailiffs, *The Rivals* and *The Agreeable Surprise'.*

Twenty years and many visits later, David Fisher confirmed his standing in the town by building a permanent theatre on the corner of Magdalen Street and Cross Street. The site in Magdalen Street, on which had once stood a brewing house belonging to the former Queen's Head, was purchased in May 1814. In September ten leading inhabitants, including three members of the Wythe family and John Clouting, music master, each lent Fisher £50 as a mortgage to finance the 'intended new erected Theatre or Playhouse'.[4]

The Theatre was opened 'with grat éclat' on the day after Waterloo, 19 June 1815. 'The convenience, comfort and general appearance of the house which was built from a design of Mr D. Fisher . . . are much approved. And the machinery and decorations executed by that gentleman himself are of a superior order. The Norfolk and Suffolk Company of Comedians are highly respectable . . . the pieces performed were *The Hangman* and the farce *Love Law and Physic'*.[5] The 1815 season was from 18 June until 8 August with performances starting at 6.30 p.m. on Mondays, Wednesdays, Thursdays and Saturdays. In a similar season at Bungay in 1799 the Company performed over 22 nights; 14 comedies, 2 tragedies, 2 plays, a drama, and a comic opera, as their main pieces, each accompanied, in a double bill, by one of 17 farces, musicals, pantomimes and romances.

The local nobility and gentry patronised the theatre, including Lord and Lady Henniker of Thornham, Sir Edward and Lady Kerrison of Oakley Park, the Dowager Duchess of Chandos of Major House, Thwaite; Mr and Mrs Wythe of Park House and Chandos Lodge; and the Bailiffs and Burgesses of Eye.

In its heyday the Norfolk and Suffolk Company of Comedians based its tours on a circuit of thirteen towns in East Anglia where David Fisher had his own Theatres. The Company travelled between these towns, carrying its impedimenta in two or three large wagons, each drawn by six horses. In the 1840s there was a country-wide recession in the theatre business, and in March 1844 the decision was made to dispose of all the Fisher Company's playhouses including the Theatre at Eye. It was purchased in 1849 by Robert and Henry Bishop, Chemists and Grocers of Eye, and the ownership descended from their half shares in the property.[6] The Theatre continued in intermittent use until the early 1870s, and it had certainly closed by February 1879, when the Corporation unsuccessfully attempted to purchase '. . . the site of the Theatre' for a Cattle Market.[7]

In July 1889 Mr Jessie Lawrence, a furniture dealer, purchased both half shares in the property, and had it demolished soon afterwards. A furniture warehouse had been built on the site by at least 1894.[8] Sometime between 1916 and 1922 the warehouse and adjoining properties became Station Road Garage (French's) which closed in 1987.

When the White Lion was sold in 1987, the Assembly Room was converted into the Somershey Theatre which housed the smallest professional theatre in the country. It opened its doors on 6 May 1988 and after a run of unique and distinctive productions, closed at the end of 1990. Early in 1991 the director Tom Scott bought the building which reopened in May 1991 as the Eye Theatre. The plays offered are varied, of a very high standard, and attract audiences from a wide area.

Notable Houses

This section seeks to draw attention to a few of the more obviously interesting houses. Full details of all the listed buildings can be found in 'The Department of the Environment: *List of buildings of special, architectural or historical interest in the Borough of Eye,'* published in 1971.

The Guildhall: a half-timbered building dating from the late 15th century. It may have been part of the property bequeathed 'for the good of his soul' by John Upson c.1488. The building was restored in 1875,[1] and little remains visible of the original structure, except for an internal tie beam; a bracket under one of the side windows; and one of the figures of the Archangel Gabriel on the corner post. In the early 18th century the antiquarian Tom Martin, recorded that the arms of de la Pole and Burghersh were carved on one of the window sills.[2] He also recorded the arms on Hill Cottage Lambseth Street, showing the Burghersh lion flanked by a lion and a chained stag. The central oriel window, against the churchyard, has the arms of Sir Edward and Lady Caroline Kerrison, and the gable window the arms of Eye. Eye Grammar School was situated in the Guildhall from c.1495–1965.

Old Vicarage: The building was enlarged by Rev. John Burgate 1723–4, by the addition of the long wing facing the churchyard. The Rev. Dr. William Broome remodelled the building by inserting new windows and doors in 1733.[3] Broome, a minor poet, collaborated with Alexander Pope, in translating Homer's *Odyssey* in 1725.

Stayer House: on the south side of Castle Street near the church is 16th century with a late 18th-century front. In about 1600 it was called 'Fetchetts' and was for many years the home of the D'Eye family whose ledger stones may be seen in the church. In the 19th century part of this building was used as a private bank, and during the Second World War it was used as a home for the elderly.

Stanley House: in Castle Street, was built about the middle of the 15th century as a hall house. In the early part of the 20th century, and probably long before this, it was a private school. For about thirty years until 1978 the house was lived in by Cavendish Morton, an artist, who was Mayor of Eye several times and who gave his time and effort generously to work in the town. There is a crinkle-crankle wall dividing the garden from the former stables.

Harwen House: a large, brick, gabled house in Castle Street. At an unknown date an annual rent-charge of £2 10s was bequeathed from this property, to be distributed at Christmas to 'poor widows and maidens in Eye'. During the early part of the 20th century the house contained a large dressmaking and millinery business which employed quite a number of women from the town.

The Red House: near the Town Hall in Lambseth Street, is 18th century and was owned by doctors for many years, with a surgery in part of the house. In the 1950s the third storey was removed leaving a flat roof and rather spoiling the appearance of the house. For many years before, this house was the home of the Tacon family, many of whose memorial stones can be seen in the cemetery. The Tacons owned the large brewery nearby, where Tacon Close now is. Charles Tacon (d.1909), who lived in the White House, was Mayor of Eye for ten successive years and his brother Sir Thomas Tacon (d.1922) was Mayor of Eye for eight years. Sir Thomas Tacon bequeathed £700 to the Borough in 1910, the interest from which was to provide coals to the poor, in January and February each year.[4]

The White House: in Lambseth Street has also been used as a school. The school was started by Miss Gambril in 'Nature's Garden', the greengrocer's shop in Church Street, and eventually moved to the White House in about 1929. Miss Winterton ran the school there until the early 1950s. Many people living in Eye today went to this school. The house has subsequently been converted into flats.

Chandos Lodge: behind the crinkle-crankle wall on the corner of Lambseth Street and Castleton Way. The house was designed in 1811 by Dent Hooper of Chelmsford, for John Wythe Jr., and called Chandos Lodge after his wife's great-aunt, Elizabeth Duchess of Chandos. The house was occupied by the late Sir Frederick Ashton, the famous dancer, choreographer and Director of the Royal Ballet 1963–70, until his death in 1988. The building has a late 18th-century central range of brick stuccoed over, and lined to look like stone blocks, with an early 19th-century wing either side.

Linden House: set back behind a row of limes in Lambseth Street. The house was built in the late 17th century, and was encased with a red brick classical skin in the early 18th century.

For about thirty years, until the late 1950s, this house was occupied by six unmarried sisters called the Misses Thompson. All of them were professional women, mostly teachers, and two were involved in the suffragist movement. Margaret Thompson, who was a militant suffragette, had three spells of imprisonment with Mrs Pankhurst and Mrs Pethwick-Lawrence between the years 1909 and 1912. Mary and Margaret published their memories of this period in 1957 in a small book entitled *They couldn't stop us!*

Broad Street, c.1880; note the lamp post which was removed in 1888 for the Kerrison Memorial; the Police Station lamp on the corner of Magdalen and Broad Streets, and the group of men outside the White Lion. The shop in Broad Street with three windows in the gable belonged to Otto Rands, basket and sieve maker who ceased trading 1879–83.

The Eye Volunteers

The Eye Volunteers were formed in April 1798 in response to the threat of invasion by Napoleon.[1] They agreed to meet at Langton Green for two hours training three days a week, at their own expense. The Volunteers had a band from their early days. In June 1804 the Corps, which had been under the command of Captain John Wythe of Park House since 1798, was inspected by Col. McLeroth, Inspecting Field Officer for West Suffolk '. . . when after passing in review order and going through the manual and platoon exercises, the Corps went through many of the 18 manoeuvres, much to the satisfaction of the Colonel, who commended the Corps for their steadfastness under arms, and the manner in which they went through the different evolutions, which he was pleased to say were done exceedingly well and that the Corps was equal, and in marching in line superior, to any Corps within his inspection.'[2]

Between 1803 and 1812 the annual inspection returns show that, on average, Captain Wythe was in command of 3 Subalterns, 5 Sergeants, 2 Drummers and 95 rank and file.[3] The Corps was disbanded along with all the other Volunteers in 1812.

The Eye Rifle Volunteer Corps (10th Suffolk) was enrolled in January 1860, and later became 'B' Company of the 2nd Volunteer Battalion of the Suffolk Regiment. The Town Hall was used as the Drill Hall, and a rifle range was set up on the Town Moors. It is interesting to note that in the Tudor period, butts for archery practice had been established on the Moor. In 1908 the Volunteers became a detachment of 'A' Company of the 5th Suffolk Battalion of the new Territorial Force, which in turn became part of the Territorial Army in 1920.

Eye Territorial Detachment, c.1912.

Eye in the 1890s

The 1896 County Directory, like the whole series between 1844 and 1937, gives details of the institutions and organisations in the Borough of Eye, including the following extracts. The additions in brackets are from earlier Directories.

Corporation: Charles Tacon, Mayor; Henry Gedny, Deputy Mayor; 4 Aldermen; 12 Councillors; Town Clerk; Treasurer; Medical Officer of Health; Borough Surveyor and Inspector of Nuisances; Sergeant-at-Mace; School Attendance Officer; and Town Crier.

Courts: Petty Sessions for the Borough are held every Saturday at the Town Hall; for Hartismere Petty Sessional Division every alternate Monday; the County Court under Judge H. Eardley-Wilmot every alternate month.

Places of Worship: The parish church of St Peter and St Paul is a large structure of flint with stone dressings . . . in 1868–9 the chancel was restored by the late Sir E. C. Kerrison and the rest of the church by subscription . . . The living is a vicarage . . . 14 acres of glebe and residence, in the gift of Lady Bateman (daughter of Sir E. C. Kerrison) and held since 1893 by Rev. Arthur Spencer. There are 800 sittings; services at 10.30 a.m. 3.00 p.m. and 6.30 p.m.; and 11.30 a.m. on Wednesday and Friday.

The Wesleyan Chapel in Castle Street was erected in 1877, and has 120 sittings; services at 2.30 p.m. and 6.00 p.m.; and on Tuesdays fortnightly 6.00 p.m. in winter and 7.00 p.m. in summer.

The Baptist Chapel in Church Street was erected in 1810 and rebuilt in 1863; services at 10.30 a.m. and 6.30 p.m.; and at 8.00 p.m. on Monday and 7.30 p.m. on Thursday.

Markets and Fairs: The Corn Market and Town Hall, which occupy the site of the old building, were opened 12 May 1857. The market is on Monday for corn, and a fair is held on Whit Monday for pleasure. A fortnightly sale of cattle is held close to the railway station by Messrs Bond, of Ipswich.

Cemetery: The Cemetery on the Ipswich road, originally of two acres was laid out in 1856 but in 1889 it was enlarged by the addition of two acres of land adjoining, a cottage being at the same time built as a keeper's lodge; there are two mortuary chapels, and the whole is under the control of a Burial Board of nine members.

Post Office: Post, Money Order, Telegraph Office, Savings Bank, Annuity and Insurance Office in Broad Street; Arthur Till, postmaster. Letters delivered at 7.00 a.m., 12.45 p.m. and 6.20 p.m. Wall Letter Boxes in Castle Street, Churchgate and Railway Station.

Railway: A line of railway (opened 1868) joins the main line at Mellis to this town, passing through Yaxley; it is worked by the Great Eastern Company. Harry Unwin, station master.

Police and Fire Engine: County Constabulary for Eye District at Broad Street, Superintendent, a sergeant and two constables. Fire engine in Magdalen Street.

Hartismere Union: The workhouse, a building of red brick, at the east end of the town, is available for 320 inmates; there are now 112 inmates; the children are sent to the training school at Wortham. Lester Barling, master.

Charities: Bedingfield Almshouses (see earlier section).

William Small: 1654, rent-charge of £10 from Eye Park for the apprenticeship of poor boys born in Eye.

William Woodman: 1572, rent-charge of £3 6s 8d on lands at Cranley paid to the Parish Clerk of Eye.

Thomas Herring: c.1635, a farm of 42 acres at Old Newton, rent to provide coals for the poor.

Thomas Hilton: 1640 rent-charge of £1 12s from Town Farm.

Harwin: date unknown, rent-charge of £2 10s from house called Harwin House in Castle Street.

Ann Lowmax: 1641, rent-charge of £1 from Bull Inn (Lambseth Street).

These three last charities are distributed to the poor in the form of tickets for which groceries and other goods may be obtained from the tradesmen of Eye.

Apart from these charities administered by groups of trustees, were Kent's and Mallow's charities for the Grammar School, and the following charity houses and lands, administered as one trust: 14 acres called Bush Croft in Scole (1408); house and 134 acres of land in Cranley (1498); site of a house called Gestas in Cranley (1466); Foddismere meadow in Eye Moor (1479);

2 acres called Cooking Stool Meadow in Eye; the Guildhall and yard; 28 acres called Task Lands in Cranley, 6 acres in Mill Field in Eye (1500); 20 acres in the Moor, 2 cottages in Magdalen Street (1575, one was sold to the Gas Company, and the other converted into the Fire Engine House); the Town Hall; and 2$^1/_2$ acres in Hoxne.

Schools: The Grammar School rebuilt mainly through the generosity of the late Sir E. C. Kerrison was enlarged in 1878, and in 1882 a large dining hall was erected; the headmaster's house was completely restored in 1876 by Lady Caroline Kerrison; the buildings now consist of school and classrooms, master's house, dining hall, library, boys' bedrooms and sanitorium. Special arrangements are made for weekly boarders. There is also a large meadow for recreation. Mr William Watkins is the headmaster. The present chairman of the governors is the Rt. Hon Lord Henniker.

National School, Castle Hill, for 300 boys and girls, and 100 infants, average attendance 182 boys and girls and 84 infants. (School built by Sir E. Kerrison in 1839, and an Infants' Department added in 1848; Sir E. C. Kerrison paid for further additions in 1859, 1871 and 1876). Frederick Bray master (1888–1921), Miss Rosa Eagleton infants' mistress (1889–96).

Banks: There are two branch banks here, Barclays and the London and Provincial, both in Broad Street.

Gas Company: The town is lighted with gas from works (in Magdalen Street) belonging to the Eye Gas Light and Coke Co. and supplied with water from private wells.

Foresters, Odd Fellows and Freemasons: A lodge of Foresters meets at the Black Swan Inn, one of Odd Fellows at the Three Horse Shoes, and the Hartismere Lodge of Freemasons at the White Lion Hotel.

Volunteers: 2nd Volunteer Battalion Suffolk Regiment (B Company). Drill Hall at Town Hall (formerly the Eye Rifle Volunteer Corps, enrolled in January 1860, and in 1874 had 120 men). Major Francis Woolnough, commanding.

Medical Club: The Medical Club, founded in 1876, numbers between two and three thousand members.

Lady of the manor: Lady Bateman of Brome Hall, daughter of the late Sir Edward Kerrison, is Lady of several of the surrounding manors and proprietor of the greater part of the land.

Area and Population: The area is 4,100 acres; rateable value £7,913; the population in 1891 was 2,064, including 107 officers and inmates of the workhouse.

Broad Street looking towards Castle Street, c.1880. The lamp standard is dated 1851 and has a list of distances from Eye to various towns and villages.

Jubilee Dinner, 21 June 1887, on The Paddock. 1,200 adults and children sat at 60 tables for the meal provided by the Town Council. Eye Volunteers Band, centre left; Day's builders yard in background; Fishers' Brewery to right.

The Inter-War Period

The main developments in the period 1918–39 were the provision of public services and utilities which included housing, water, sewage, street lighting and telephones, and in 1931 the closure of the Eye to Mellis Railway for passengers.[1]

Housing: In 1919, as part of Lloyd George's drive to create 'homes fit for heroes' the Borough Council became responsible for the provision of Local Authority Housing. Between 1919 and 1930 the Borough built 50 homes, the first of which were the two pairs in Magdalen Street in 1921.

The former workhouse had been adapted into seven temporary homes by March 1920. In 1924 Hooper and Garrard, architects of Ipswich, converted the old east facade into six modern-style 'town houses'. Each had a living room and kitchen on the ground floor, and two bedrooms on the first and second floors.[2] Between 1922 and 1928 a further six houses were built to the west of the facade. In 1979 the entire site was cleared and the new curving range of 20 houses erected in 1980, the first tenant moving in during January 1981.

The first 16 houses at Victoria Hill were built as 'parlour' and 'non-parlour' dwellings in 1921–2. As a result of slum clearance in 1935–6, a further 6 houses were erected. The original 16 dwellings were demolished and replaced by Elizabeth Way and Elizabeth Court 1982–4.

Further slum clearance gave the impetus to begin the Castleton Way development of 12 dwellings in 1937. Four more dwellings were added to the site in 1963.

Water and Sewage: Plans for providing a domestic mains water supply from local boreholes, and mains drainage and sewerage works began in 1936. The site for the sewerage disposal works, near Waterloo Plantation, was purchased in 1938, and the pumping plant installed in 1940. The water in the water tower was declared fit for human consumption in 1940. However, both schemes were suspended until after the war, and the conversion of earth to water closets continued well into the 1950s. The water undertaking was sold to the East Anglian Water Company in 1963.

Lighting: Gas street lighting and some domestic lighting has been provided by a private company since 1850. To prevent the closure of the Gas Works the Borough Council purchased the company in 1922, and continued the provision of gas until 1939. The East Anglian Electric Supply Company brought electricity to Eye in 1933, although they do not seem to have provided street lighting until 1945.

Telephones: There had been telephones in Eye since 1907, but the only public phone was at the Post Office, telephone number Eye 1. In 1932 the Post Office erected the first street kiosk outside the Town Hall, and in 1934 the first automatic exchange was installed in Wellington Road.[3]

Charity lands: In the 1920s many of the charity lands which had formed part of the Borough income since the Reformation, and were administered by the Borough Treasurer, were sold. These included the Town Farm at Cranley, part of which had been bequeathed in 1498, and land in Scole and meadows in Eye bequeathed by Robert Anyell in 1479.

Miscellany: Other items of interest in this period, not mentioned elsewhere, include the sale in 1922 of the 'Pest' or 'Pocky House', now called 'Appletree Cottage', which had been used to isolate sufferers from infectious diseases since at least the early 19th century; the formation of Eye Cricket Club c.1925–9, although the earliest recorded match was in 1768; the formation of Eye Badminton Club in 1933; the building of the Co-operative store in Church Street in 1933; and the resolution of the Council '. . . in favour of the proposed Channel Tunnel' in February 1929.

Eye Area School

Area Schools were a pioneering venture in the provision of secondary education in the 1930s. The 90% of pupils, who did not obtain a place at a Grammar School, remained at their Elementary School from 5 to 14 years of age. A Government enquiry of 1926, called 'The Education of the Adolescent' (The Haddow Report) recommended that these pupils should have secondary education.

In 1929 East Suffolk County Council decided to implement the Haddow recommendations and provide senior elementary schools for pupils aged 10½ to 15 years. These Area Schools were to serve pupils from a surrounding group of elementary schools. The original intention was that pupils should not have to travel more than 4 miles to school, and could be lent cycles and waterproof capes.

The Area School curriculum emphasised the 3 Rs, practical subjects, craft work, games and leisure interests such as gardening, music and reading. Class subjects, such as history, geography and science, were to be made relevant to the interests, experience and abilities of the pupils. The H.M.I. report for 1931 stated '. . . that only in East Suffolk was the real Haddow scheme being put into practice . . . The whole keynote is practical instruction from beginning to end.'[1] In 1933 the Board of Education publicised the East Suffolk Area School scheme in one of its educational pamphlets.[2]

Eye was selected as a site for an Area School in 1930. The proposal was to close the Grammar School, extend the accommodation from 100 to 250, and reopen as Eye Area School.[3] As a result of strong local opposition, in 1933 the Authority decided to build a new school in Castleton Way. The school opened in September 1935 with 230 children drawn from Eye, Occold, Brome, Mellis, Yaxley Thrandeston, Thornham, Thorndon and Stoke Ash. The school, designed by Mr E. J. Symcox, the County Architect, was officially opened in July 1936 by Mr Oliver Stanley, President of the Board of Education.

The single-storey school was built around a quadrangle, and originally had six classrooms; Domestic Science room; Handicraft and Science room; canteen for school lunches, and assembly hall. The playing fields amounted to 3 acres, with a further 3 acres of gardens as a 'school estate' with vegetable, flower gardens and experimental plots. From the outset it was the aim of Mr Henry Ford, the first Headmaster, to make the school a centre for evening social, educational and leisure activities, which has continued to the present day, with the addition of sports facilities.[5]

After the 1944 Education Act the school became Eye Secondary Modern, and served a wider catchment area. As a result of Comprehensive reorganisation the school became Hartismere High (11 to 16 years) in September 1979. Extensive additions were built including the Sports Hall for school and community use. It is proposed that the school will have a Sixth Form in 1995.

Magdalen Street, c.1910. Charles Beales, coal merchant and gas works on left.

Church Street, c.1920; A. J. Day, pork butchers' shop on right.

The Second World War

Life in Eye during the war has been vividly recalled by Dorothy Presswell, an evacuee from 1939–45, in her book *A Sparrow in the Meadow* (1985), and the impact of American airmen and airfields on the area in *A Miscellany of Memories* by the Pattemore Pen Pushers (1992).

In September 1939 Sandringham Road Central School, East Ham, London, was evacuated to Eye, and the staff and pupils billeted on local families until July 1945. The evacuee pupils were taught as a separate unit at the Area School, where they were made welcome by the Headmaster Henry Ford and his staff. From May 1940 the junior children and their teachers occupied a classroom at the National School.

At 4.00 p.m. on 11 September 1940 a German Dornier 17 plane dropped three bombs on Eye, none of which exploded, and strafed part of the town with machine gun bullets. One bomb fell outside the Town Hall, and bounced into a bedroom of Nunn's the Outfitters which was opposite. Another version of the events says the bomb hit a lorry delivering to Nunn's shop, and ricochetted into the open bedroom window.[1]

Herbert Adams, Headmaster of the National School, trained the children in Air-Raid Drill, and noted in May 1940 that the school had been cleared and the shelters occupied in two minutes. He also recorded the May air-raid, and several other air-raid warnings in October 1940. Throughout 1941 he carefully noted the times of the warnings, which were most frequent from January to April, but rarely allowed them to interrupt the school timetable, preferring to 'continue lessons in school'.[2]

Fire watching was carried out from the clock room of the Town Hall bell tower, where clear glass was inserted in the clock face at the half hour. The Home Guard and War Agricultural Committee had their offices in Broad Street. Hartismere Hospital became Eye Emergency Hospital, with a resident surgeon and doctor; the operating theatre was in what is now the occupational therapy room. Chandos Lodge was used as a convalescent home for wounded servicemen. Italian prisoners of war worked on farms in the locality including Burnt House Farm at Eye.

In 1943 construction of a class 'A' heavy bomber airfield was begun at Eye, by the U.S. Army Engineer Battalions 827 and 859 and British contractors, and was completed early in 1944. It consisted of three intersecting runways, two large hangars, administrative buildings, and enough living quarters for 2,894 servicemen. The base housed Station 134 of the 490th Bomb Group of the U.S. 8th Air Force which operated Liberators and Flying Fortresses. Between May 1944 and April 1945, 158 missions and 5,060 sorties were flown from Eye. The aircraft left Eye on 8 July 1945 and the remaining ground crew departed in August. The base was handed over to R.A.F. Bomber Command in November 1945, gradually run down and decommissioned in 1961. Eye Church was on the approach to one of the runways and in consequence had a red hazard light fixed to the tower.[3]

A black Regiment, the 932nd Regiment of Aviation Engineers was responsible for the maintenance of the base. Eye was off-limits to white servicemen on certain evenings, and to black servicemen on others. In 1984 the White Lion, and the experiences of local people, formed the basis of a T.V. programme called *Jim Crow's Army,* about black servicemen in England during the war.[4]

Members of the 490th Bomb Group Veterans, the 'Eye Guys', returned to celebrate the 40th anniversary of the airfield in 1984, and donated a shelter at Brome and a collection of books to the High School. In 1992 they returned again to both Brome and Eye to commemorate the 50th anniversary of the 'friendly invasion' by the U.S.A.F. At Eye on 29 June, the Duke of Grafton took the salute at the parade before the Memorial Service at the parish church.

The Post-War Period

The main developments in Eye since the war have been the building of Bellands Way, Castle Hill, Elizabeth Way, Highfield, Haygate, Gaye Crescent, Hutton Court, Posting House Court and Millfield; the provision of sheltered accommodation at Tacon Close and Elizabeth Court, and a retirement home at The Paddocks; the development of the former station and airfield as industrial areas, bringing employment to the area; the conservation of the Town Moors; the provision of purpose-built Fire Station, Library, Health Centre, Community Centre and town centre Car Park.

There have also been major changes in the structure of local government which resulted in the loss of Borough status; changes in education resulted both in the closure of the Grammar School and the creation of the High School; changes in the delivery of local services led to the loss of many of those services.

Housing: In 1943, as part of the Government's Post-War Housing Scheme, the Borough proposed to develop the Bellands Way Estate of 40 houses on a seven-acre site. The estate, which was originally designed by Mr Scott-Moncrieff of Horham, grew to meet the increasing housing need between 1947 and the 1970s. The first 14 houses were completed by November 1948. The large grass area was first sown in 1953, and swings erected in 1966.

The name was chosen in 1949 from the field, now occupied by houses 76–137 in Ash Drive, called Belland. The name suggests that it was originally bequeathed in order that the income could be used to repair the church bells.

In 1963 Mr K. M. Kenworthy designed two pairs of houses to fill the gaps at Castleton Way, the numbers 15–16 and 23–24 were built the same year.

In 1960 the Borough asked East Suffolk County Council to consider Eye as a site for a Residential Home for the Elderly. The County Council owned land in Church Street called 'The Paddocks' and in 1964 Paddock House was opened.

In 1926 the Borough had purchased the site of the Colchester Brewery in Lambseth Street, which was later leased to Hartismere Rural District Council. In 1970 the Borough proposed building sheltered accommodation on the site. Tacon close, named after Maud, Charles and Thomas Tacon, with 14 bungalows was opened in 1975 and has recently been extended.

In 1965 the Borough housing stock stood at 50 pre-war and 66 post-war dwellings. By 1986 the total number of dwellings owned by Mid-Suffolk District Council had increased to 206, comprising 134 houses, 51 bungalows and 21 flats.[2] As we saw earlier 20 dwellings at Castle Hill were built in 1980, and the 16 houses at Victoria Hill built in 1921–2, were demolished and replaced by Elizabeth Way, and Elizabeth Court sheltered accommodation in 1982–4.

Private housing estates have been developed since the 1960s. The first of these were Highfield and Haygate in the mid-1960s and Gaye Crescent in the early 1970s. The Millfield estate around the site of the former Victoria windmill in Castleton Way was built in the early 1990s.

Industry: In 1958 the Borough Council invited London firms to establish light industries within the Borough, but with little response. Pollastra Packers, now Sovereign Chicken, began negotiations for the erection of a Poultry Packing Station on the old sale ground at the former Station in Magdalen Street in 1959. Planning permission was granted in 1960 and the firm has steadily expanded ever since, to become one of the largest employers in the district. In 1977 the firm became part of the Favor Parker Group which employs 2,000 people in East Anglia and sells its products widely in the U.K. and northern European markets.

When the former airfield was decommissioned in 1961 the Council applied for part of the land to be scheduled for industrial and residential development. The first firm to occupy the site was Stramit Boards of Stowmarket in 1962. They were followed by A. Moor and Sons in 1966 and Mill Farm Mushrooms in 1970. British Gas erected a Gas Compressor Station on the airfield in 1975.

Europe's first commercial Power Station using poultry litter as a fuel was opened by Fibropower in June, and began generating electricity on 19 October 1992. The electricity provided by this 'environmentally friendly' process provides Eastern Electricity with sufficient power for 12,500 homes.[3]

Library and Fire Station: A subscription library and reading room had been established at the Town Hall since at least 1840. The membership was drawn from the upper and middle classes of the town. In order to extend this facility to working class men, Sir E. C. Kerrison built a Working Men's Club in 1867. The building, still remembered as the Reading Room, in Lambseth Street was near the entrance to the recently destroyed Flax Works, and on the site of the present Fire Station. Sir Edward's intention was that the Club should be an alternative place of recreation to the public houses, and provided with tea, coffee, games, newspapers and a lending library to which he gave 100 books.[5] The Headmaster of the National School recorded '. . . 6 Feb. 1867. The books for the Working Men's Hall were covered in the school.'[6]

In 1982 Mr Charles Etheridge recalled that '. . . the front room was the Billiard Room, and the large room at the back was the Parish Room where Whist Drives, Socials, Dances, Clinics, and other meetings were held. At the end of this was a small room, the library, where members could have two books out for a week free of charge, and non-members paid 5s a year. Outside there were two quoit beds where members played . . .'.[7] In 1964 the building was sold to the Ipswich and East Suffolk Fire Authority, demolished and a new Fire Station was built on the site in 1965. This replaced the Fire Engine house in Magdalen Street, which had been in use since at least the 1870s.

In 1947 a Branch Library of the East Suffolk County Library had been established in the Magistrates' Room at the Town Hall. This facility remained until 1973 when the new purpose-built library was opened in Buckshorn Lane.

Public Convenience: The provision of this much needed facility was first proposed in 1945. The suggested sites, however, in Cross Street, next to the Town Hall, in the old Brewery Yard, in the former Black Swan, and behind the Reading Room were all opposed and eventually rejected. Finally the waiting room and cells at the Sessions' Hall, which closed in 1962 were converted into a public convenience which opened in 1967.

Car Park: Car parking became an increasing problem in Eye as elsewhere in the 1960s. A car park in Buckshorn Lane was proposed in 1969, which necessitated the demolition of No 1–3 Buckshorn Lane and No. 8 Church Street, The car park was officially opened in 1971. Yellow line street parking restrictions came into force in March 1974.

Other significant events which have not been mentioned elsewhere include the erection of Lambseth Street Bus Shelter by the Coronation Committee in 1956; Castleton Way Bus Shelter in 1962; the closure of Eye County Court in 1962; the construction of Hartismere R.D.C. offices in Castleton Way in 1966; Meals on Wheels service started in 1968; Eye Bowls Club formed in 1969, and a Green laid in 1970; Eye Conservation Area established in 1970; Eye Playgroup started in 1973; Eye Bach Choir founded in 1974; Methodist Church closed in 1977; Scout Hut opened in Wellington Road in 1979; Primary School extensions dedicated by the Bishop of Dunwich in 1979; the construction of the Health Centre 1979–80; former Methodist Church opened as Gospel Centre linked to the Assemblies of God Church at Diss 1979–86; Sewerage works started in 1980; Eye and Diss Citizens Advice Bureau opened in 1981; Eye Arts Guild founded in 1982; Eye Cricket Club became owners of Old Grammar School Field at Ludgate in 1983; Noncomformist Cemetery Chapel closed in 1983; Registrar's Office at Victoria Hill closed in 1987; Eye Catchers Ladies Cricket Team founded in 1987; Eye Ambulance Station closed in 1989; Eye Baptist Church and Diss Covenant Church united to form the Vine Church in 1990; Gospel Centre re-opened as an Evangelical Church in 1992; Methodists from Eye and Mellis began to use the Gospel Centre on alternate Sunday afternoons in 1992.

Eye in the 1990s

Having declined after the main line railway went to Diss, Eye has in recent years seen something of a renaissance. It is one of those rural centres that was just of sufficient size to expand, and become more of a focal point upon the decline in recent times of the English village. Although overshadowed by Diss, Eye has survived as a vital service centre for education and health because the two towns are in different counties.

Eye now has a wide range of shops, offices and services, a High School, a Primary School, a Public Library, a Theatre, two Public Houses and a Restaurant. There is a Geriatric Hospital, a Maternity Unit and a Health Centre sharing the same site in Castleton Way, a Fire Station in Lambseth Street, a Police Station in Victoria Hill and a Garage in Lowgate Street.

A splendid new Community Centre was completed in 1991 on the Town Playing Field. Eye and District Cricket Club have their own pavilion and pitch on the old Grammar School playing field, off Ludgate Causeway. There is a Bowls Club, a Youth Centre, a Residential Home for the elderly and two groups of Council owned Sheltered Accommodation. There is also a Town Hall, Anglican Church, a Baptist Chapel, a former Wesleyan Methodist Chapel now the Gospel Centre, a Scout Hut, a Red Cross Centre and an Opportunity Centre for the Mid-Suffolk Volunteer Bureau, the Opportunity Playgroup and the Toy Library.

Eye is a very active town in which there are many interest groups including a Bach Choir, an Arts Guild, several sporting associations, a Women's Institute, a Cub and Scout group and a Playgroup. There are many charitable organisations such as the British Legion, the Red Cross Society and the Eye and District Blind Committee. Save the Children Fund and St Elizabeth's Hospice are among the charities which receive regular support in Eye. There is also a Crime Prevention Panel and a Citizens Advice Bureau. The Woodland Society takes care of the woodland part of the Moors and there is an excellent Borough magazine which is distributed free each month to every house in Eye.

The High School and the Library are used for adult education courses. A Women's Institute market is held every Wednesday in the Town Hall. A small Market survives at the Cross on Mondays and on most Sundays in the year there is a Market on Eye Airfield. The annual Eye Show which is held during the August Bank Holiday weekend, and is the successor to the former horticultural show which started in the late 19th century, attracts thousands of visitors to the town.

The particular charm and interest of Eye lie in the fact that, without being sleepy, it has managed to preserve the atmosphere of a small 18th and 19th-century market town. It lies off main roads, is sufficiently remote from large cities not to be a significant commuter centre, and its failure to expand and industrialize in the 19th century has meant that the historical character of the town has been maintained.

Town Twinning

Hartismere High School has been operating an annual exchange with the Collège of Antoine de St. Exupéry in Pouzauges since 1979. As a result of this successful relationship Eye twinned with Pouzauges in the Vendée in France. There were two Easter twinning ceremonies, in Pouzauges in 1988 and in Eye in 1989, when charters and gifts were exchanged. The Fire Brigades in each town also exchanged charters and gifts in separate ceremonies. The twinning has flourished and grown with the formation of many friendships and frequent visits, both formal and informal.

The start of the Single European Market was marked at midnight on New Year's Eve 1992, with a beacon at the bottom of the castle mound, and the firing of red, white and blue rockets.

Notes

Abbreviations

HMC Historical Manuscripts Commission
N&NRO Norfolk and Norwich Record Office
PSIA Proceedings of Suffolk Institute of Archaeology
SRO(B) Suffolk Record office (Bury St Edmunds branch)
SRO(I) Suffolk Record Office (Ipswich branch)

The Name and Site of Eye

1. Ekwall, Eilert, *Concise Oxford Dictionary of English Place-Names* (1960) 171; and Scarfe, Norman *Suffolk in the Middle Ages* (1986) 3.
2. Leyland, John, De Rebus Britannicis Collectaneorum, Vol. 3, 23–24, in Horn, Thomas (ed) *Joannis Lelandi Antiquarii de Rebus Britannicis Collectanea,* Vol. 4 (1770) 26.
3. Scarfe, Norman, *The Suffolk Landscape* (1972) 152.
4. Coppinger, W. A., *The Manors of Suffolk,* Vol. 3 (1909) 262.
5. Leyland, John, *op. cit.,* 23–24.
6. Domesday Book entry for Hoxne, fol. 376r.
7. Dugdale, Sir William, *Monasticon Anglicanum,* new edition by John Caley et al, Vol. 3 (1821) 404–5. For an English summary of the foundation charter see Brown, Vivien, *Eye Priory Cartulary and Charters,* Suffolk Record Society: Suffolk Charters Vol. XII, part 1 (1992) 12.
8. Domesday Book, Eye, fol. 319v.

Archaeological Finds

1. *PSIA,* Vol. 35 (1981–4) 156.
2. Moore, Ivan; Plouviez, Judith and West, Stanley, *The Archaeology of Roman Suffolk* (1988) 54.
3. *East Anglian Notes and Queries,* Vol. 1 (1864) 249; and Page, William (ed), *Victoria County History of Suffolk,* Vol. 1 (1911) 305.
4. *Ipswich Journal,* 19 May 1781; and Page, William (ed), *ibid.,* 305.
5. Suffolk Archaeological Unit Index of Finds.
6. *Gentleman's Magazine,* 1818, 131–3; and *Proceedings of the Society of Antiquaries,* Vol. 3 (1856) 186.

Norman Eye

1. Domesday Book, Happisburgh in Norfolk, fol. 133v; and Chediston, fol. 332v.
2. Hollister, C. W., Henry I and Robert Malet, in *Viator* IV (1973) 115–22 and Lewis, C. P., The King and Eye: a study in Anglo-Norman politics, in *English Historical Review*, 412 (1989) 569–87.
3. Domesday Book, Eye, fol. 319v.
4. Rackham, Oliver, *Ancient Woodland* (1980) 121.

Eye Castle

1. Leyland, John, *op. cit.,* 23–4.
2. Domesday Book, Hoxne, fol. 379r.
3. *PSIA,* Vol. 34 (1978) 218.
4. *PSIA,* Vol. 37 (1991) 267.
5. Colvin, H. M. (ed), *History of the Kings Works,* Vol. 2 (1963) 649.
6. *PSIA,* Vol. 36 (1988) 317.
7. Colvin, H. M., *op. cit.,* 649.
8. *Ibid.,* 649.
9. *Ibid.,* 649.
10. *Calendar of Patent Rolls,* 1215, 146a.
11. *Ibid.,* 1317–21, 218.
12. Fox, John, *Ecclesiastical History, containing the Acts and Monuments of Martyrs* (1610), 1735 & 1740.
13. Leyland, John, *op. cit.,* 23–4.
14. Tom Martin's notes on Eye, 18th century SRO(I) HD225.
15. Eye Town Book 'C', fol. 5v–6r: SRO(I) EE2/E/2.
16. David Davy, *Journal of Excursions Through the County of Suffolk 1823–44,* Blatchly, John (ed), Suffolk Record Society, Vol. 24 (1982) 234.

The Honour of Eye

1. *Red Book of the Exchequer,* H. Hall (ed.), Rolls Series, Vol. 99 (1897) 92.
2. *Calendar of Inquisitions Post Mortem: Edward I,* 604.
3. *Calendar of Patent Rolls, 1313,* Part 1 3d.
4. *H.M.C. Report on the Manuscripts of the Corporation of Eye,* 10th Report, Appendix part 4 (1885) 513 and MacCulloch, Diarmaid, *Suffolk and the Tudors* (1986) 24.
5. Suit Rolls of the Tourn 1594–1787, and 1707–82: SRO(I) HA 414: Boxes 22–4.
6. Tom Martin's notes on Eye: SRO(I) HD 225.
7. Castleward Rents, 1743: SRO(I) HA 411: Box 27 No. 10.
8. *Rotule Hundredorium, 1275,* 148 and 193.
9. *Calendar of Close Rolls,* 1381–5 and 1401.

10. Certificate, 1445: SRO(I) EE2/L8/1: also printed in HMC., Report, *op. cit.,* 517.
11. For details of the Lords of the Honour, see Brown, Vivien, *op. cit.,* part 2.
12. Grant of Honour, 1697: SRO(I) EE2/T/3.
13. Henning, B. D. (ed), *House of Commons 1660–90,* Vol. 1 (1985) 134.
14. State of the Honour, c.1689: SRO(I) HA 85: 3144/14.
15. Deed, 4 Nov. 1500: in Tom Martin's notes on Eye, SRO(I) HD 225.

The Church of St Peter and St Paul

1. For example, Robert Hardyng gave £1 in 1470: SRO(B) Baldwyn 457; William Hubert £6 13s 4d in 1473: N&NRO, 1 Hubert; William Seaman £2 13s 4d in 1475: SRO(B) Hervye 43.
2. Will of William Cakyrmoll 1477: SRO(B) Hervye 171.
3. Will of John Cullyng 1487: SRO(B) Hervye 384.
4. British Library: Egerton Roll 8779; quoted in Richmond, Colin, *John Hopton, A 15th Century Suffolk Gentleman* (1981) 163.
5. Eye Town Book 'Z': SRO(I) EE2/E/3 fol. 23v; also printed in HMC, Report *op. cit.,* 531.
6. Will of Robert Anyell, 1479, in Eye Town Book 'Z' fol. 12–14.
7. Pevsner, Sir N. B. L., *Buildings of England: Suffolk* (1974) 206.
8. Tom Martin's Church Notes: SRO(B) E2/41/8A 202 fol. 202.
9. Will of Sir John Porter, 1501: N&NRO, 59 Popy.
10. Gunn, S. J., *Charles Brandon, Duke of Suffolk c.1484–1545* (1988) 54 and Plate 6 and Gunn, S. J., and Lindley, P., Charles Brandon's Westhorpe, an Early Tudor Courtyard-House, in *Archaeological Journal,* Vol. 145 (1988) 279 and Plate XX.
11. Correspondence re Rood Screen, Dec. 1868–Feb. 1869: SRO(I) FB135/E2/20.

The Priory of St Peter

1. Dugale, Sir William, *op. cit.,* 404–5.
2. Brown, Vivien, *op. cit.,* part 1, No. 9, 12 and 26.
3. *Taxatio Ecclesiastica . . . Pope Nicholas* (1291) 123, and *Valor Ecclesiasticus* (1535) Vol. 3, 476–7.
4. Fairweather, F. H., 'Excavations on the site of the priory church and monastery of St Peter, Eye'; in *Antiquaries Journal,* Vol. 7 (1927) 299–312.
5. *Calendar of Fine Rolls,* 1377–83, 129.
6. *Calendar of Patent Rolls,* 1381–85, 491.
7. *Valor Ecclesiasticus, op. cit.*
8. *PSIA,* Vol. 8 (1894) 105–8.
9. *PSIA,* Vol. 36 (1988) 324 and plate 20; and Fairweather, F. H., *op. cit.,* 310.
10. MacCulloch, Diarmaid, *op. cit.,* 60.
11. Harper-Bill, C., Church and Society in Twelfth Century Suffolk, in *PSIA,* Vol. 35 (1984) 207.

The Red Book of Eye

1. Leyland, John, *op. cit.,* 23–4.
2. James, M. R., 'The Sources of Archbishop Parker's Collection of Manuscripts at Corpus Christi College Cambridge', in *Cambridge Antiquarian Society, Octavo Publications,* No. 32 (1899) 6–7.
3. Brown, Vivien, *op. cit.,* part 2, B. L. Mss. Egerton 3140.
4. HMC, Report, *op. cit.,* 536.

The Seal of Aethelwald

1. Gurney, Hudson, 'Observations on the Seal of Ethilwald, Bishop of Dunwich', in *Archaeologia,* Vol. 20 (1824) 479–83.

Eye Park

1. *Calendar of Patent Rolls,* 1313 part 1. 3d.
2. *Inquisitiones ad quad domnum,* 1314, 151, and HMC, Report, *op. cit.,* 518.
3. *Calendar of Close Rolls,* 1329, 34.
4. *HMC Report on Salisbury Manuscripts,* part 2, 188.
5. *Exchequer Special Commissions,* 1590, 38, Appendix, 46.
6. *Report of the Commissioners for Inquiring Concerning Charities in Suffolk* (1824–40) 272.
7. *East Anglian Miscellany* (1930) 31 No. 8171.

Charter and Borough

1. Constitutions 1566: SRO(I) EE2/B/7.
2. Charter, 1575: SRO(I) EE2/B/2; and Constitutions, 1579: SRO(I) EE2/B/10/3.
3. Charman, D., *The Strange Case of the Eye Charter,* Typescript of a public lecture at Eye 27 April 1959. In possession of Jan Perry, Local History Recorder for Eye.
4. *Calendar of Patent Rolls,* 1334–8, 418.
5. Charter, 1408: Essex Record Office, D/DBy/Q19.
6. Borough Court, 1420: SRO(I) EE2/F/1.
7. Deed, 5 June 1457: SRO(I) EE2/M2/13.
8. Will of Robert Anyell, 1479, in Eye Town Book 'Z': SRO(I) E2/E/3 fol. 12–14.
9. Additional Charters: 16567: British Library.

10. Eye Town Book 'Z' fol. 30r.
11. Confirmation of Charter, 1559: SRO(I) EE2/B/1 and account of charges in Book 'Z' fol. 20v.
12. Dunwich charter, in SRO(I) EE2/B/10/3.
13. Chamberlains accounts 1547–8: SRO(I) EE2/L1/4i.
14. Constitutions, 1566 and 1579: SRO(I) EE2/B/7 and EE2/B/10/3.
15. Charter, 1697: SRO(I) EE2/B/4 and transcript EE2/B/10/2.
16. Grant of Arms, 1592: SRO(I) EE2/C/1.
17. Eye Town Book 'B': SRO(I) EE2/F/1 fol. 40r.
18. Grant of transfer of Arms, 11 March 1976. SRO(I) EE2/C/2.

Roads in the Borough

1. Eye Court Leet, 1595: SRO(I) EE2/F2/1.
2. Eye Corporation Minute Book, Bye Laws, 1819: SRO(I) EE2/J/1/7.
3. Eye Borough Council Minute Book: SRO(I) EE2/J/1/12.
4. Charles Etheridge, *Memories of Eye,* unpublished manuscript (1982) copy with Jan Perry.

The Town Moor

1. Eye Borough Council Minute Book (1919–39): SRO(I) EE2/J/1/14.
2. Eye Borough Council Minute Book (1952–74): SRO(I), EE2/J/1/16.
3. *Evening Star,* 29 September 1988, and *East Anglian Daily Times,* 5 December 1990.
4. *East Anglian Daily Times,* 28 March 1990, and 18 September 1991.

Elections and Patronal Families

1. MacCulloch, *op. cit.,* 26 and SRO(I) EE2/B/14.
2. Cobbett, William, *Rural Rides,* Everyman edition (1912) Vol. 2 220.
3. *Bury and Norwich Post,* 24 May 1843.
4. Busby, J. H., *My Lord's Borough: A Parliamentary History of the Borough of Eye,* unpublished typescript, 1975. Copy with Jan Perry.

The Cornwallis Family

1. Storey, Gertrude, Culford Hall, in *People and Places* (1973) 150.

The Kerrison and Bateman-Hanbury Families

1. Tithe Survey of Oakley: SRO(I) FDA184/A1/1; Denham: FDA83/A1/1a; Eye: FDA92/A1/1a; Brome: FDA24a/A1/1a; Hoxne: FDA138/A1/1a; Yaxley: FDA304/A1/1a.
2. *Public Men of Ipswich and East Suffolk* (1875) 35.
3. SRO(I) HD78:2671, Brome.
4. SRO(I) SCO74/2.
5. *Eastern Daily Press,* 1 October 1958.

The Market Place

1. Domesday Book, Hoxne, fol. 379r.
2. Will of Stephen Gissing of Eye, 1725: SRO(B), IC500/2/80 fol. 294.
3. Eye Tithe Apportionment, 1839: SRO(I) FDA92/A1/1a.
4. Eye Chamberlain's Account 1542: SRO(I) EE2/L1/4n.
5. Eye Town Book 'B': SRO(I) EE2/E/1 fol. 35v.
6. Chamberlains Accounts 1589: SRO(I) EE2/L1/5.
7. Eye Borough Council Minute Book, 1838: SRO(I) EE2/J/1/8.
8. Eye Assembly Book, 23 September 1653: SRO(I) EE2/I/1 and, Treasurers Accounts, 1653–4, EE2/L2/5/6.
9. Constitutions, 1579: SRO(I) EE2/B/10/3 sections 11–14.
10. Court of the Clerk of the Market 29 November 1675: SRO(I) EE2/I/2.

The Town Hall

1. Eye Borough Court Book 1451–59: SRO(I) EE2/F2/1.
2. Chamberlains Account 1590: SRO(I) EE2/L1/5.
3. Constitutions 1579: SRO(I) EE2/B/10/3.
4. Deed, 12 August 1608: SRO(I) EE2/M1/5/2.
5. Lease and Inventory, 20 October 1634: SRO(I) EE2/M1/9/13.
6. Eye Assembly Book, 1649: SRO(I) EE2/I/1.
7. N&NRO: COL/7/11.
8. Eye Borough Council Minute Book, 25 February 1840: SRO(I) EE2/J/10.
9. Eye Borough Council Minute Book, May 1856: SRO(I) EE2/J/1/11.
10. Eye Borough Council Minute Book, July 1856 and April 1857: SRO(I) EE2/J/I/11.
11. Town Hall Committee, July 1856: SRO(I) EE2/N1/1.
12. Brown, C., Haward, B., and Kindred, R., *A Dictionary of Architects of Suffolk Buildings 1800–1914* (1991) 136–7.
13. Pevsner, *op. cit.,* 208.
14. *Suffolk Chronicle,* 21 August 1856 and 16 May 1857.
15. Eye Borough Council Minute Book, May 1887: SRO(I) EE2/J/1/12.
16. Design for bell turret by George Leighton of Ipswich: SRO(I) EE2/N/3; and Borough Minutes, 9 November 1897: EE2/J/1/12.

17. Raven, J., *The Church Bells of Suffolk* (1890) 189.

The Gaol

1. Deed, 12 August 1608: SRO(I) EE2/M1/5/2.
2. Lease, 20 October 1634: SRO(I) EE2/M1/9/13.
3. Eye Borough Council Minute Book, 16 April 1818: SRO(I) EE2/J/1/7.
4. *Reports of Inspectors of Prisons, Northern District,* 10 December 1835, 97.
5. *Report on Municipal Corporations* (1835) Vol. 4 2229–32.
6. Eye Borough Council Minute Book, July 1837: SRO(I) EE2/J/1/8.

Workhouses

1. Eye Town Book 'B': SRO(I) EE2/E/1 fol. 54v.
2. Eye Assembly Book, 1649: SRO(I) EE2/I/1.
3. Eye Overseer's Accounts: SRO(I) FB135/G1/3&4.
4. *Ipswich Journal* 31 August 1793 and Legal Opinion by Queen's Council, 1835: SRO(I) EE2/Q2/11/1.
5. *Abstract of Answers and Returns re the Expenditure & Maintenance of the Poor in England* (1803) 480–81.
6. Legal Opinion: SRO(I) EE2/Q2/11/1.
7. *Report to Poor Law Commissioners on the Administration of Hartismere Union* (1838).
8. *Bury and Norwich Post*, 15 February 1837.
9. *Ibid.*, 22 March 1837.
10. White, William, *Directory of Suffolk* (1844) 321.
11. Stacpoole, J., *William Mason, the first New Zealand Architect* (1971) 16–17.
12. White, William, *Directory of Suffolk* (1855) 584.
13. Hartismere Union, Guardian's Minutes: SRO(I) ADA3/AB1/3.
14. *Ibid.*
15. Eye Borough Council Minute Book: SRO(I) EE2/J/1/13 503 and 508.
16. Eye Borough Council Minute Book: SRO(I) EE2/J1/14.
17. Plans to convert workhouse into houses, 1924: SRO(I) EE2/V/6.

Magdalen Hospital

1. Calendar of Patent Rolls 1329 and 1337, quoted in Page, W., *op. cit.,* Vol. 2 138.
2. Will of Jacques Blondell, 1492: N&NRO, 134 Typpes.
3. Eye Chamberlains Account, 1458: SRO(I) EE2/L1/2.
4. Lease, 1604: SRO(I) EE2/E/2 fol. 7.
5. Book of Eye Charities: SRO(I) EE2/M5/1.

Bedingfield Almshouses

1. Deeds, 1621: SRO(I) EE2/M1/6/11 and EE2/M1/9/26.
2. Will of Nicholas Bedingfield, 1636, quoted in Charity Book: SRO(I) EE2/M5/1.
3. *Ibid.*

Grammar School and Guildhall

1. Eye Town Book 'A', 1452–9: SRO(I) EE2/F2/1, also quoted in Chancery Case, 1841: EE2/M4/1/3(33).
2. Will of John Fisk, 1488: N&NRO, 51 Typpes, also transcribed in Eye Town Book 'Z': SRO(I) EE2/E/3 fol. 2.
3. Eye Town Book 'Z', fol. 8 & 9; also printed in HMC, Report, *op. cit.,* 527–8.
4. *Ibid.,* fol. 22.
5. Chantry Certificate, 1547 in *PSIA* Vol. 12 (1906) 31 and 46.
6. Leaf, Elfrida, *History of Eye 1066–1603.* Unpublished M.A. thesis, University of Leeds (1935) Chapter 3, p41: SRO(I) q S Eye 9; copy also in possession of Jan Perry.
7. Chantry Certificate, 1547, *op. cit.*
8. Book 'Z', fol. 21.
9. Book 'Z', fol 36, also printed in HMC, Report, *op. cit.,* 533.
10. Constitutions, 1566: SRO(I) EE2/B/7, sections 74–8.
11. Eye Assembly Book 'R', 27 September 1650: SRO(I) EE2/I/1, printed in HMC, Report, *op. cit.,* 534–5.
12. Will of Francis Kent, 1593; printed in *Charity Commissioners Report* (1830) 268.
13. Eye Town Book 'B', 1599: SRO(I) EE2/E/1 fol. 29.
14. *Ibid.,* fol. 30.
15. Will of Edward Mallowes 1614, printed in *Charity Commissions Report* (1830) 270.
16. Eye Assembly Book, 1672: SRO(I) EE2/I/2, fol. 8.
17. *Ibid.,* fol. 8.
18. Letter of Protest 1681: SRO(I) EE2/M1/3/6.
19. Eye Treasurers' Account Book, 1719–96: SRO(I) EE2/L2/3/1.
20. Appointment of John Knevett, 1822: SRO(I) EE2/Q2/11/7.
21. *Charity Commissioners Report* (1830) 269.
22. *Schools Inquiry Commission* (1867) 167–9.
23. *Bury and Norwich Post,* 25 May 1875.
24. *Ibid.,* 29 February 1876.
25. Eye Grammar School Minute Book: SRO(I) 172/1.
26. *Diss Express,* 22 December 1911.
27. *Eye Grammar School Prospectus* (c.1930) SRO(I) S Eye 373.

28. Eye Primary School Log Book: SRO(I) FB135/M1/2/6.

Occupations and Industries

1. Blome, Richard, *Britannia* (1673) 213.
2. *Post Office Directory of Norfolk and Suffolk* (1865) 678.
3. Caulton, Geoff, 'Suffolk Lace', in *Lace: the Journal of the Lace Guild,* Vol. 26 (1981) 16, and *East Anglian Daily Times,* 26 June & 2 October 1981.
4. Notes on History of Eye, by Miss E. H. Bugg of Church Street (1930s) in possession of Faith Legg.
5. *Bury and Norwich Post,* 3 January 1865.
6. *Bury and Norwich Post,* 21 September 1888.
7. Eye Town Council Minute Book, 2 January 1850: SRO(I) EE2/J/1/9.
8. Eye Town Council Minute Book, February 1922: SRO(I) EE2/J/1/14.
9. Eye Corporation Gas Works Minute Book, August 1939: SRO(I) EE2/J/3/9.

Breweries and Public Houses

1. Constitutions 1566: SRO(I) EE2/B/7, section 28.
2. Eye Borough Court Book 'M', 1529–1631: SRO(I) EE2/F2/2/3.
3. *Ipswich Journal,* 31 January 1801.
4. David Davy Collections for the History of Suffolk; Hartismere Hundred, British Library Add. MMS. 19091. Microfilm SRO(I) J400/5&6.
5. *Bury Post or Suffolk Mercury,* 1 January 1739.

Communications

1. Robertson, Alistair, 'Turnpikes and Stage Coaches' in Dymond, D., and Martin E., *An Historical Atlas of Suffolk* (1988) 104–5.
2. Pigot's *Directory of Suffolk* (1839) 548; and White's *Directory of Suffolk* (1844) 335.
3. Eye Borough Council Minute Book, 21 March 1846: SRO(I) EE2/J/1/10.
4. *Bury and Norwich Post,* 22 November 1864.
5. Acts, 28 and 29 Victoria, cap. 249 (1865).
6. *Ipswich Journal,* 6 April 1867.
7. Two detailed histories of the line are, Joby, R. S., *The Mellis and Eye Railway* (1977): and Paye, P., *The Mellis and Eye Railway* (1980).
8. *Borough of Eye Magazine,* October 1985.

Fairs

1. Borough Constitutions, 1566: SRO(I) EE2/B/7, section 27.
2. Eye Borough Court Book, 1590–5: SRO(I) EE2/F2/2/1.

The Theatre

1. *Ipswich Journal,* 11 September 1784.
2. Field, Moira, *The Lamplit Stage: The Norfolk and Suffolk Company of Comedians 1794–1844* (1985) gives a detailed history of the company.
3. *Ipswich Journal,* 7 September and 2 November 1793.
4. Deeds of Theatre: SRO(I) HD 348/1806.
5. H. R. Eyre, 'Material for a history of Suffolk Theatres': SRO(I) qS 792, p.106.
6. Deeds of Theatre: SRO(I) HD348/1806.
7. Borough Council Minute Book, 12 February 1879: SRO(I) EE2/J/1/12.

Notable Houses

1. *Bury and Norwich Post,* 25 May 1875.
2. Tom Martin's Church Notes: SRO(B) E2/41/8A/fol. 195.
3. Colman, Sylvia, 'Eye Vicarage' in *PSIA,* Vol. 34 (1977) 49–58.
4. Borough Council Minute Book, 9 November: SRO(I) EE2/J/1/13.

The Eye Volunteers

1 .Resolutions of Eye Volunteers, 18 April 1798: SRO(I) EE2/P18/1.
2. *Ipswich Journal,* 16 June 1804.
3. Letter Book of Lord Lieutenant of Suffolk 1803–14: SRO(B) HA513/5/144 & 5.

The Inter-War Period

1. Eye Borough Council Minute Books: SRO(J) EE2/J/1/15 and 16, contain all details in this section.
2. SRO(I) EE2/V/6.
3. Cawston, John, Telephones in Eye, in *Borough of Eye Magazine,* July 1985, 25.

Eye Area School

1. *East Anglian Daily Times,* 19 December 1931.
2. *An Experiment in Rural Reorganisation,* Board of Education Pamphlet No. 93 (1933): SRO(I) 1452/1.
3. *East Anglian Daily Times,* 19 November 1930 and 11 March 1931.
4. *East Anglian Daily Times,* 29 November 1933.
5. *Eastern Daily Press,* 22 July 1936 and SRO(I) 1439/2.

The Second World War
1. *Borough of Eye Magazine,* April 1984 and June 1984.
2. Eye National School Log Book: SRO(I) FB135/M1/2/2.
3. Freeman, Roger, *Airfields of the Eighth* (1978) 84–5; and *Norfolk and Suffolk Journal,* 9 November 1984.
4. *East Anglian Daily Times,* 4 December 1984.

The Post-War Period
1. Eye Borough Council Minute Books: SRO(I) EE2/J/1/15 and 16, contain all details in this section.
2. 'Domesday Survey of Eye': SRO(I) T4616.
3. *Evening Star,* 24 September 1990; *East Anglian Daily Times,* 2 August 1991; *Borough of Eye Magazine,* June and July 1992.
4. Eye Borough Council Minute Book, 25 February 1840: SRO(I) EE2/J/1/9.
5. *Bury and Norwich Post,* 5 February 1867.
6. Eye National School Log Book: SRO(I) FB135/M1/2/3.
7. Etheridge, Charles, *op. cit.*

General Index

NOTE: Maps and illustrations are indicated by a **bold page number.**

Index of Contemporary Names

NOTE: Maps and illustrations are indicated by a **bold page number.**

White Lion Yard

Eye National School, Class 4; 1920